Sex and the Single Grandma

Sex and the Single Grandma

LYNN S. GARSON

GREENE GARNET

PUBLISHING

First printing May 2019

Sex and the Single Grandma paperback edition: 978-0-9859500-2-6
Sex and the Single Grandma e-book edition: 978-0-9859500-3-3

For inquiries:
S Creamcheese, LLC
Attn: Lynn Garson
27 Ridgemere Tr.
Atlanta, Georgia 30328

www.lynngarson.com

CONTENTS

INTERLUDE

PART FIVE — RICHARD

INTERLUDE

PART SIX — ZANE

CODA

ACKNOWLEDGMENTS

This book is dedicated to my friends.

You know who you are.

PART ONE

❦

Let the Quest Begin

CHAPTER ONE

The Invisible Woman

A fter half a lifetime of marriage and a split with my husband, Wayne, at the ripe age of fifty-three, anger was my dominant reaction, followed by fear, then sadness, and finally, hope. What if someone wonderful was out there, my very own Sir Lancelot? In the best of all possible worlds, this knight in shining armor would be raven haired, broad in the chest, and own—not rent—his horse.

Let the quest begin!

Eager to assist, my friends set me up with the single men of their acquaintance, though these were paltry few. There is some hidden algorithm whereby, in the universe of baby boomers, for every single man there are at least thirty single women, and of those men, a maximum of three are known at any one time to any one woman's friends. Fortunately, we have the corollary principle that every vacuum exists only to be filled and hence, the birth and proliferation of the online dating services that we have come to know and love/hate so well. Thanks to the efforts of these friends and the diligence of my online activities, dates were plentiful. To my growing puzzlement, however, the men I dated all had one thing in common. Far from raven-haired knights, I found myself adrift in a sea of white hairs, bald heads, or at best, graybeards, all of whom bore an uncanny resemblance to my grandfather.

On the plus side, the opportunity to visit with doppelgängers of my long-dead grandpa was welcome. Grandpa had been a memorable guy, with a dashing old country accent and manners to match.

On the minus side, all I could think was, "What the hell?"

My last date had been with Wayne twenty years earlier, right before we became engaged. At the time, like most men in their late twenties, every hair on Wayne's head, not to mention his body, was intact and jet black. Nothing sagged, nothing flapped, nothing wrinkled, and unflagging optimism was the order of the day. Single again so many years later, my unconscious—albeit wildly unrealistic—expectation was that both the look and the outlook of the men I dated would be unchanged.

Ah, there was the crux of it. Time, cruel jester that she is, had tricked me. As long as Wayne and I had been growing older together, we were like two trains moving along parallel tracks at the same speed—neither seemed to move at all. But send one train down a divergent track, and suddenly perspective returns, unforgiving and harsh as a phosphorescent flare.

For a long while, railing against an uncaring universe that had failed to prepare me for such a blow, I was prickly, insensitive, and not altogether stable[1]—perhaps not the best person to date during that time. A few years and some instructive encounters later, I became more accustomed to the new world order and accepted that, yes, my dates were older men and life had happened to them, leaving its mark. Inescapably, I was older, too, with my own battle scars, some visible and some hidden. So be it. And what about these men? Did they, upon re-entering the dating pool after years coupled up, find themselves similarly in need of adjusting their view of women?

Posing the question in a support group I had long attended provoked a spirited discussion, which ended abruptly when the therapist leader commented, "Well, you know, women over fifty are invisible."

Pop quiz: Was the therapist a man or a woman? You guessed it—a man. Likely he was speaking not only for the legions of men out there, but also for himself. It was not a kind thing to say, and certainly elicited an outraged response from the women in the group, but it also made me wonder about my own search for romance. Was it doomed from the start?

---

1 Can you say "euphemism?"

Walking down the street, standing in line to order my lunch, wherever I happened to be, I began to pay attention. Were men looking? What drew their eyes? Who were they watching? Newsflash: It wasn't me. Dress as I might, apply the latest mascara until my eyes were practically glued shut, put to use dating advice rendered by one and all, it didn't matter. Men—young, old, fat, thin, hirsute, no suit—did not spare me a glance. Talk about harsh reality. A woman over fifty really did seem invisible, absent buckets of money or aging good looks like Sophia Loren (who, notably, also has buckets of money).

Was I thus condemned to a life devoid of romance? At first, it certainly looked that way. But no, for every rule there is an exception. As time went on I found that for some men, yes, I was invisible, but for others, apparently I was there in glorious living Technicolor.[2] There was a whole flotilla of men who could see me. They could pick me out of a crowd in the dark wearing sunglasses. They could find me inside a titanium-lined vault buried fifty feet underground in the desert. In a tree, in a car, in a scree, in a bar, up or down, in the country, in a town, in a wood, they could find me, Sam I Am. Oh Dear Lord, yes they could.[3]

Who were these superheroes?

---

2 What would be the modern equivalent? 3D digitized virt ual reality with every filter known to mankind? Suddenly everybody's an artist. Thank you, Mr. Jobs. I think.

3 In an abundance of caution, let me hasten to attribute my rhyming diatribe to that genius and idol of my childhood, Theodor Geisel, or "Dr. Seuss," as he was known. Remember *Green Eggs and Ham*?

(a) They were men who fell through the cracks, hit hard in the Great Recession of 2008 in the graying years of their lives. Jobless, divorced, widowed, wedged into small apartments or ensconced in the crumbling family home, they were hurting.

(b) Many were looking for a woman, not just any woman, but a woman to whom they could entrust the task of putting their lives back together. It became the duty of the women who came into their lives to bring these lost sheep back from the margins into the fold, into the community, into the world, into life. To make plans for them, find friends for them, decorate houses for them, and create activities for them.[4]

(c) Such men had a knack for finding me. As a mother-lawyer-author-advocate-pet-owning-Nice Jewish Girl, they saw me as a likely candidate.

Looks can be deceiving. It's trouble enough keeping my own ox out of the ditches, much less anybody else's. So, to all of you and your brethren—tall, short, thin, fat, black, white, other-ethnic, sixty-year olds, seventy-year olds, eighty-year olds(!), devout, non-believer, gourmet, gourmand, esthete, ascetic, biker, musician, analyst (both kinds), doctor, lawyer, butcher, baker, or candlestick maker, whoever you might be, let me say this: look elsewhere. Please.

---

4 Unless these beleaguered men wanted to pull their dilapidated circumstances around them like Linus' blanket. You'll meet one such man shortly.

Don't know who Linus is? Sick of these blasts from the past already? Hah. Just wait.

Lest this come across as "Poor Me" or perhaps "Conceited Bitch Me," let me be clear: my defects are legion. My plusses and minuses are equal and in some strange, Jungian way, practically synchronized. Examples abound. Many friends call me the dumbest smart person they have ever met. Sometimes what comes out of my mouth is so dumb it has to be heard to be believed. Match that with the fact that my vocation of many years has been practicing law for nationally recognized law firms, an attractive hire based on my status as both Law Review and Order of the Coif,[5] and you'll get an idea of one dichotomy that I am. To boot, I am high maintenance and easy going; by turns Southern belle and feminist; entitled and down to earth; the model of sanity and instability; selfish and generous; self-centered and empathetic; steadfast and skittish; intuitive and unobservant; seductive and withdrawn; an open book and a closed door; often independent and—buzz kill of all buzz kills—occasionally needy. All true, at times and by degree.

Small wonder that my quest for Mr. Right has had some pitfalls and that some of the men I have dated have turned out to be Mr. Wrong. This book is the story of several such, written because sometimes you just have to laugh. It is also the story of a Southern woman born in the 1950s who drank the Kool-Aid and still believes in Love, Romance, and Happily Ever After, even if the sound of the clock ticking is becoming *really* loud.

---

5   The Order of the Coif is awarded to those students who graduate in the top ten percent of their law school class. Law school was one of my better eras.

PART TWO

Allen

CHAPTER ONE

---※---

The Curly Tail Grub
and Other Lures

After many months of frustratingly bad dates, finally a winner appeared, so I thought. A champion, the Charles Atlas of the dating pool.[6] This man was caring, bright, witty, funny, and clever. He was older, seventy-five to my fifty-seven, but who cared? An older man was perhaps wiser; this was probably a good thing. He might find a place in my life not as a father so much as a mentor,

---

6 If you've never heard of the weightlifter Charles Atlas, think Arnold Schwarzenegger, before he gained admission to higher society and embarked upon questionable governance, then sank back into the role of beefy action hero.

someone to admire and provide strength. Besides, my mother was in her grave smiling away. She had always wanted me to marry an older man, a sophisticated roué who had sowed his wild oats, made his fortune, and finally was ready to settle down. George Clooney, to be precise. Question: Do I now or did I ever resemble Amal Clooney in any way? Not a bit. Never a socialite, I have always kept a low profile on purpose. Facts, though, never did trouble my mother or inconvenience her in any way.

Unlike previous contretemps, I knew Allen for almost eight months before we had a date. Through much of that period, though he was on my radar, there wasn't much time to think about him or find out if he was available. My law practice occupied most of my time and the rest was spent in volunteer activities or on the congested roads of Atlanta, shuttling back and forth between home and office. At least it was April and the azaleas were in full bloom, their lush colors competing for attention from the senses with the glorious smell of hundreds of magnolia blossoms. Growing up, our driveway was lined with magnolia trees, an even dozen down either side, which, even as a child, never failed to inspire awe.

Allen had his own law firm in a town not too far away, still actively practicing at seventy-five, and we were on opposite sides of negotiations on business deals from time to time. In addition to four of five face-to-face meetings, we had spoken at length on numerous occasions over the previous eight months on client matters, and often segued into personal asides and funny stories. Perhaps he, like most of the interesting men I came across, was married, and just enjoyed the banter for its own sake.

About seven months in, Allen casually dropped the word "JDate," that is, "Match.com" for Jews.[7] As a lure, it was akin to a Curly Tail Grub or a Dardevle Spinnie, for those fishermen out there. Like any self-respecting wide mouth bass, I bit. Single *and* Jewish? Irresistible.[8] A week or two later, when Allen responded to an email about our client negotiations with a gallant, "anything for you, dear lady," we were in business. After a few days, I asked whether he would like to get to know each other over drinks after our next scheduled meeting. He was delighted, "Love to, can't wait! Where and when?"

We set up a date for the afternoon after our next business conference, about two weeks hence. The time came, and after wrapping up our work, we waved goodbye to our respective clients and headed off to the bar in the downtown Atlanta Ritz Carlton, near my office. Small minded as it sounds, part of me thought, "OK, this is good. He likes to go to nice places and seems to do well enough not to mind paying for a ten-dollar drink."

Do not judge. This was not so much small minded as the culmination of a hard won, extended, post-divorce process of working to convince myself that I was worthy

---

7 Having fallen victim to, oops, I meant to say joined, both Match.com and JDate at various times in my dating quest, in my estimation the primary difference is that the former encourages seduction via golf lessons while the latter promotes attraction through the fine art of casserole-making.

8 Religious affiliation is pretty much irrelevant to me, but I do have a soft spot for Jewish men, having been raised (*very* secularly) Jewish myself.

of a man of substance, in every sense of the word. At the outset, I had dated anyone and everyone, including a man who was so down and out that his memory of living in his car was more or less immediate. My choices at that time reflected my own poor self-esteem and fear of being alone. It was a measure of increased self-respect and stability that I no longer tolerated homelessness in a suitor. The bar now had been raised to: "You should be able to take care of you and I should be able to take care of me, and then we'll talk."

Allen and I sat down across from each other in comfortable brown leather chairs, flanked by two large Chinese-style oxblood urns filled with bamboo and tropical flowers. Soft music played—the Carpenters, one of my favorites. Considering the stress of both of our jobs, it was a treat to be in such a mellow environment. When Allen loosened his tie, apparently unwinding too, the mood was relaxed, with just a touch of sexual tension. So far, so good. We both ordered a drink and settled down for some "get to know you" conversation.

We talked at length about his parents, who had cut him off when he married a non-Jewish woman in his early twenties. This seems impossible today, but such stories were not uncommon forty or fifty years ago, and may still occur in some segments of the Jewish community. Soon after announcing his impending marriage to his family, Allen's mother called to say that his family had lit a "Yahrzeit" candle, the candle lit in memory of the dead. This was not a euphemism. His family in fact considered Allen dead to them and there was no further contact for many years. We discussed the pain this caused him, and the resentment he still harbored so many years later.

In the middle of our relaxed moment, we both glanced at our emails, which has become habitual these days even at our ages. One of Allen's was a mini-emergency that he jumped up to handle. As I munched on some guacamole and chips—how did I live without guac for the first half of my life?—I looked around the bar. Seated under an impressive pair of wall sconces, a couple was holding hands and talking intimately, immersed in each other. They had something I wanted and I wondered if someday that could be Allen and me. So far, he certainly seemed like a solid prospect.

Emergency contained, Allen walked back and we resumed our conversation. Among other things, we talked about my memoir, *Southern Vapors*, with me paying close attention to his reaction to the publication of my story. The book describes my journey into the depths of depression and the years of recovery that followed. It is a very open and heartfelt exposé of a difficult time, full of struggle with no holds barred. Despite being so public about my life, it feels strange to tell a prospective suitor about the book, and I feel vulnerable. While Allen was as yet closed and unknown to me, my life was an open book to him, should he choose to read the memoir. To my delight, there was no judgment on his part. On the contrary, he was warm and complimentary and more insightful than most about the revelations I had described there. That was a good sign.

Four hours after our arrival, we looked at our watches, amazed that we had been so engrossed in talk. The sixteen-year-old girl part of me cheered, "Yay, this is really good, this could be *the guy*, you know what I mean?" A more adult response would have been to question the idea that *the guy* was out there somewhere and could be identified on a first date. Then again, that whole adult thing is vastly overrated, don't you think?

CHAPTER TWO

Road Trip!

All in all, it was a very good first date that left me wanting more. And more there was, though initially not physically getting together. We called, texted, and emailed, first every few days, quickly turning into almost every day. Sometimes it was a brief check in, sometimes a long chat. Our schedules were both full for several weeks, but we agreed that we were happy to get to know each other better and excited by the thought of the next date. Allen was cute and clever, as in, "People are starting to talk about us—I know, I'm the one who started the rumors." Funny and dear, right? I responded in kind: "Don't tempt me, I might come down there and visit you one weekend."

Before you could say "Jackrabbit," that was exactly the plan we made.

Allen was stuck at home because his ninety-five-year-old mother had taken a turn for the worse. Allen and his mother (never his father) reconciled after years of banishment, soon after Allen's father died. Living in a nursing home, her health would soon require hospice care, and he didn't feel able to leave town.

This was something I understood, having gone through my father's decline a few years before. So I would travel to Allen. Road trip! Cute guy, still sexy at seventy-five! I asked if I could bring my elderly dog, Hazel, and Allen said, "Sure, I have three dogs and a cat myself!" One was a miniature Italian greyhound like the dog my family owned when I was growing up, a pet I did not recall fondly. Our little Amy mostly shivered and quaked, with the occasional whiny snort thrown in, and I didn't expect much different from Allen's dog. Since he had inherited the dog from his deceased wife, it wouldn't do to criticize him for its acquisition. Oh yes, Allen's wife had died twelve or so years earlier, which added to his status as an A+ suitor. Among my coterie of single women over fifty, a widower is prized above a divorcée, the thinking being that there is less likelihood of that certain—as the French might say, *comment dirai-je*[9]—feeling of bitterness that often follows a divorce and has been known to linger for, well, hmmm, might we say, decades?

---

9 French for "Hmm, how shall I say this?" and carrying an undertone of "this is not the easiest thing to communicate, but I can count on you, in your vast and stunning sophistication, to know what I mean, because after all, we are Frenshh, n'est-ce pas?" Sometimes nothing but the French way of saying a thing will do.

Of course, we had *the talk* before I committed to visit and stay the night, insisting on having my own bedroom. It was the usual drill:

"I just want to get to know you better."

"Let's take things slow."

"I'm not really ready to commit to anything more than a casual relationship."

"My last (hundred) dating experiences have left me gun-shy. Let's see if we can be friends first."

Everything a horny guy just loves to hear, right?

To my delight, Allen responded like the perfect gentleman. "Oh no," he assured me, "I don't want you to do anything that makes you feel uncomfortable. I have a second bedroom that I will clean up for you. Don't worry about anything, it's going to be great. I'm just so happy that you are coming!"

What over-fifty lovelorn chick is not gonna love a guy like this?

Giddy as a teenager, I tripped through the following days, humming through my work and ignoring my annoying upstairs neighbor whose resting bitch face could give Kim Kardashian a run for her money. When it came time for me to get on the road, Allen called to check on me and ask what I wanted for dinner. This was a booby-trap for the unwary. If I requested fine dining, Allen might pigeonhole me as a JAP.[10] A little entitled though I

---

10 Jewish American Princess, satisfied by nothing less than a black American Express card.

might be,[11] a JAP I am not. I pay for my own dinner while privately keeping score of every cheapskate move my date makes. A JAP, on the other hand, lets her date pay for dinner while openly and volubly judging him for every cheapskate move he makes. A fine distinction, some might say, but an important one. As a well brought up Southern female, it is axiomatic that a lady of refinement never, *ever* (a) takes a date for a ride or (b) talks in public about money. Shored up by my mother's relentless attention to "bringing me up right," side-skirting the booby trap was child's play.

Allen, the Mensch:[12] "I'm happy to take you out. Where do you want to go?"

Demure Lynn: "I'll be tired from the drive. Just pick something up and we'll eat at your house."

Allen, the Mensch: "Really? What kind of food do you like?"

Demure Lynn: "Oh, anything is fine. Don't go to too much trouble. How about something from Zaxby's? My son says their restaurants are really good."

Allen, the Mensch: "Okay, if you're sure. Zaxby's has great salads and there's one near my house."

Demure Lynn: "Sounds great; be there in a few hours!"

Allen, the Mensch: "Drive carefully, can't wait to see you!"

---

11   Don't quibble. It's unattractive.

12   Please tell me you understand Yiddish. No? Never heard the word? Oy vey. What is the world coming to? "Mensch" means a good guy.

"Oh my," I thought, "This is going to be good. What a sweetie!" The impulsive, co-dependent, needy damsel in distress who lives inside me, just waiting for moments like these, went from zero to one hundred in the space of five seconds. "This is going to work out, I can already tell, so let's plan it all out. Let's see, Allen lives about three hours away. Not good. I don't like to drive long distances. Maybe I'll move to the other side of town—that would cut at least forty-five minutes off the drive. Maybe Allen will move, too. That will cut another half hour off and we'll just be a little over an hour and a half away. Then we could even meet in the middle for lunch once in a while!"

The mature adult who also resides in me—remember her?—responded: "You jerk, you idiot, how many times have you done this? You get overeager and then you scare the guy away. You haven't even visited Allen, you don't know the first thing about him nor he about you, so take a chill pill. Right now, this minute! Think about something else, turn on the music, play with the damn dog, but stop constructing this stupid fairy tale."

The adult in me won, sort of. I turned on the music and pushed thoughts of romantic bliss out of my mind, or at least into a small cupboard under the stairs.

CHAPTER THREE

Didn't See That One Coming

The drive to Allen's house led me through a boring stretch of highway, flat and interrupted only by the occasional billboard for an "antiques mall" or lodging/food/gas. When did plates that came in boxes of Duz dishwashing detergent[13] start making the cut as antiques? It is beyond me.

---

13   For a description of Duz dishes, check out https://www.kovels.com/collectors- questions/golden-wheat-dish-set. At this writing, there was an unopened box of the detergent itself for sale on eBay for $100. No kidding. Plus $10 for shipping. As for the golden wheat dishes that came in the Duz boxes, who would have imagined their continued popularity? Clearly, not me. One lucky bidder is the proud owner of a complete set for the bargain price of $50 plus $48.74 for expedited shipping—with no other delivery option. Somebody wasn't listening in class the day they taught *caveat emptor*.

With such lack of stimulation on the road, rolling down the window for some bracing air seemed like a good idea. Ack! Not so good. Either there were a lot of cows nearby producing a boatload of methane or an industrial plant lurked around the corner. Onward ho with the windows up. An accident on the highway slowed me down, and with Hazel's two pit stops, it took a while longer than I expected to arrive at Allen's exit. Finally the green sign announcing its approach appeared. On the exit ramp, my already soaring spirits notched higher, because it was the same exit as the one for my well-to-do friends who used to live in this town—proof positive that the ship had finally turned around, that Allen must be a nice guy who was also well heeled. Siri, expressly changed for the trip to "Giancarlo," a man with a sexy Italian accent, recited directions crisply, guided me past a few strip malls, and then a left turn at the Zaxby's on the corner. Allen's house was close! Time to pull down the visor and check my makeup. Intact and ready for action: let the countdown begin.

A few more turns and a minute later, I was in a neighborhood that didn't quite meet expectations. Something must be wrong. The houses, while sizable, were a little rundown, like a girl who couldn't afford her own prom dress and wore her older sister's slightly used, slightly frayed gown. A long, straight stretch followed by another turn and the houses declined further, with paint flaking on the windowsills and the yards smaller and less well tended. When the houses became even smaller and the manicured yards turned into clay-streaked ground enclosed by chain link fences, the notion surfaced that maybe the reality didn't match my fantasy of Allen as the perfect, well-established, well-heeled suitor. "Oh hell no," retorted the other voice that clings to internal fantasies until they are beaten to death by the psychic equivalent of a steel baseball bat.

"Hey, Siri Giancarlo,"[14] I wheedled. "I know what you're doing. Stop teasing me. This is going to be like the neighborhoods back in Norfolk, a lot of crappy little houses, and then you get to the end of the street to find a magnificent home on the river, replete with dock and cabin cruiser.[15] You're such a card, Siri Giancarlo! Now stop it."

Siri Giancarlo replied coyly, "In one hundred feet, turn left onto Azalea Street."

"Wow, Azalea Street is Allen's street," I thought, "Almost there!" Trying to stay on the road, while at the same time craning my neck for the dead end where the houses got fancy, I lurched violently to the right when Siri Giancarlo announced, "The destination is on your left."

Oh no, not in a million years, no way this can be the house of Allen, the man of my dreams, my Sir Lancelot in his twilight years, my lover and companion-to-be. This is *not* happening. This is just an alternative universe that

---

14   Siri Giancarlo's name evoked in me fond memories of Agador Spartacus from *The Bird Cage*, remember him? Of course, Siri Giancarlo is a lot better looking.

15   Norfolk, Virginia was my home from 2001 to 2009, years encompassing my divorce and the really bad times that followed. My best memories are of the rivers and the ocean, which I love still.

has inserted itself at just the wrong moment; all will be right with the world in the blink of an eye. So, I blinked. Same scene. Blinked again. No change. Was that a steel baseball bat shimmering in the distance?

Because, borrowing the line that Bette Davis made immortal, the only reaction possible was, "What a dump!"[16] From the tarp covering the side yard nearest the house to the screen door hanging by one hinge, this was a world-class, incontrovertible dump, in a neighborhood that one had to admit was a little scary, somehow evoking quiet neglect and all too unquiet desperation. Even in my single-minded determination for Allen to be "the guy," no rose-colored glasses would keep my fantasy intact. Would they? Could they? No, of course not, don't be ridiculous. I wasn't that invested in this relationship, barely knew Allen. After my history of dating the down and out, no way would that happen again, no way not to take the scene in front of me for what it clearly was—the home of a man very down on his luck, to be generous. No. Never happen. Not in this lifetime. Could it?

Hmmm... Whir, whir, click, click, my mind making minute adjustments, move this tile over here, push that one into that slot, now, what do we see? In front of me was a dirt yard that looked pretty much like the others in the neighborhood, but wasn't it bigger? And how about that little statue of a cherub over there; surely that exhibited a

---

16   If you want to see sneering raised to an art form, check out Ms. Davis for this and other quotations in *Beyond the Forest,* a Warner Brothers film released in 1949.

degree of flair? Behind the chain link fence grew a lovely weeping willow, branches sweeping the ground. Allen could have owned one of those other houses with completely barren yards, but no, he chose the one with the tree. Of course. A sensitive man. Oh my, a little sign with an arrow pointing at the screen door hanging from one hinge: "Welcome Lynn!" How dear! And the house itself, isn't boxy just another word for minimalist? Sensitive *and* sophisticated. My hero.

Startling me out of my mental gymnastics, out trotted Allen, but he was a little hard to see in the midst of the three dogs surrounding him: one a tremendous Rottweiler, another some sort of botched terrier with a spiky black coat, and the third, obscuring the lower half of Allen's face, Milly, his little greyhound. Milly's almost hairless body, which seemed a little indecent, and her long tongue, which lolled out of the side of her gap-toothed mouth, gave her the aspect of a drunken pirate, momentarily distracting me. Gathering my wits enough to give Allen a tentative hug, I faked a kiss. He returned my greeting enthusiastically, all the while effervescing: "I'm so glad you're here! I was worried about you on the drive. Why didn't you check in with me? Never mind, you're here now! Come in, let me grab your bag. Hazel is such a cute dog; I didn't realize how small she was from her pictures.[17] I'm sure my guys will love her!"

---

17 Just for the record, Hazel was a short-haired chocolate lab mix, at the time a respectable thirty-eight pounds. When your frame of reference is a Rottweiler, thirty-eight pounds doesn't look like much.

Grasping the sagging door with both hands, Allen cocked his hip and swung the door wide so he could drop one hand to grab my suitcase before the door banged him in the elbow. He swung the door again, hard, the remaining hinge groaning in protest, and nudged me over a fractured threshold and into the house. Tripping a little over the threshold's uneven edge, the floor required a topographical map to make sure there was nothing else to snag my sexy, not-quite-stilettos.[18]

Uncertainly wobbling about, I stopped. In. My. Tracks.

Mental gymnastics or no, how could anyone make sense of what I saw? It was like the story told of how Native Americans reacted upon Columbus's arrival in the New World. They had never seen a ship before, so they didn't see those of the Spanish as they sat anchored in the harbor. Didn't see them at all. The ships were invisible to the Native Americans because they had no visual frame of reference, no context into which their minds could place the scene that they beheld.[19]

After a few seconds, the jumble of shapes that scaled the wall almost to the ceiling resolved themselves into piles of books. Piles and piles and piles of books. Strips of wallpaper pulled haphazardly away from the wall just below the dirty beige molding. The linoleum underfoot

---

18 What presumptive Cinderella doesn't willingly sacrifice ambulation in favor of sex appeal?

19 A number of sources such as Reddit judge the story of the Native Americans a myth, popularized by the movie *What the Bleep*. If so, it's a worthy myth and ought to be true, which is good enough for me.

was sixty years old if it was a day, and the squares that were intact were streaked with grime. Several squares were missing entirely, revealing the subfloor underneath. By comparison, the rattle of the avocado-colored refrigerator freezer was reassuring; at least it sounded like it was working.

On the kitchen counter two boxes from Zaxby's sat with plastic knives and forks atop them. For some reason those sad little boxes made the kitchen look even worse to me.

Chattering away, Allen got a water bowl for Hazel out of the cabinet. The bowl was stained and had a brown crack running down one side—old glue from the look of it. Silently apologizing to my dog, I poured her some water, shoved aside stacks of old magazines and made a space on the kitchen counter for the flat of clementines and the sunflower I'd nursed through the drive from Atlanta. The orange of the clementines and the deep yellow of the sunflower brought some much-needed color into the otherwise drab and overflowing room.

In the deeply divided way I have of managing my thoughts, part of my mind said, "Leave now? Can I do that?" Yet unimaginably—idiot—my mouth opened and said to Allen that I had brought one sunflower for him and kept one in Atlanta for me, so when we weren't together, we could think of each other. I'm an idiot and a moron besides.

That earned me another hug and a kiss that landed on the corner of my mouth. Meanwhile, I continued to gather my thoughts, toting up reasons to stay and reasons to go. Heading out of the kitchen with Allen to deposit my suitcase in the guest room, I considered the fact that Allen and I did business deals together and had both recently agreed to serve on a committee of mutual interest. The committee met once a month, so that would cause us to be thrown together frequently, not to mention a current transaction that required a good deal of contact. Obviously, leaving on the heels of my arrival would make it uncomfortable to work together. Besides, I wasn't a good enough actress to pull off "Oh my God, I just got a call from my mother—she is sick and I have to go home! Call you later, bye!"

More important, the guy's predicament tugged on my heartstrings. Allen was a smart man, who put on quite the show in public but in private was falling apart. The clutter of his surroundings no doubt reflected the confusion in his mind. Wearing a mask in public was something I had done most of my life, and I knew what it represented: fear of not measuring up, of always being on guard, of rarely allowing anyone inside one's defenses. How could I not feel empathy for him?

Plus, I was attracted to him. *Really* attracted to him. Altogether, a part of me hung on to the notion that this might turn out okay. Does "dolt" sound fitting at this juncture?

For the moment, putting doubts on hold was the path of least resistance, so I ignored the voice in my head that was screaming "Reasons to go, reasons to go, hello, anybody home?"

I stayed.

CHAPTER FOUR

———— ✿ ————

Sex in the City

Allen beckoned me to follow him to the back of the house. Passing through a short hallway that was dark and narrow, we came to two facing doors. His bedroom was clearly on the left, full of dark furniture including a massive sleigh bed made up in black and gold. Large as the bed was, a tall, wide cabinet dominated the room, stretching almost the length of the wall opposite the bed. The wallpaper was as dark as the furniture, almost black. It was more than a little creepy, so why the involuntary frisson of sexual tension when looking at that bed? I knew, of course. It wasn't that complicated; I wanted to have sex.

My body parts still worked pretty much like they used to—estrogen replacement therapy is the bomb—and my desire strangely had increased, not decreased, with the passage of time.[20] It had been too long since those desires had been satisfied.

Allen pushed open the opposite door and motioned me into what turned out to be the guest room. Quite unlike the other rooms, it looked welcoming and was relatively uncluttered, containing only a double bed covered with a cozy white chenille bedspread. A matching nightstand and chest of drawers of blonde wood added to the effect, all brightened by cheerful floral curtains. Perhaps this room was a relic of Allen's wife's tenure. He put my suitcase down with a thud—I don't travel light under any circumstances—and put his arms around me. "I'm so glad you're here and we've got a whole weekend together."

He followed the hug with a long, slow, succulent kiss that wiped away the sight of his kitchen and creepy bedroom. Already turned on by the view of Allen's bed, I returned his kiss with mounting passion. It was magnificent to feel warm and tingly after so long without sex, to anticipate the beginning of the long, slow dance, knowing that a full blown lusty encounter was right there at my fingertips. The part of me that was still thinking realized that

---

20 My old nanny, Ruth, informed me not too long before this book was published that for women, "the desire for sex goes up in your seventies and eighties." She was eighty-six when she said it. Her word is gospel, so if I were a guy, I'd be putting a reminder note on my calendar to check Lynn out in ten or fifteen years.

having sex with Allen wasn't a matter of casual interest. Oh no. I longed for it, was dying for it, prodded by the memory of my last seriously good orgasm with a lover.[21] That ravishing, engorging, blood thumping experience had been a while back, right after my divorce, the Holy Grail of sex. If there was even a shred of possibility of that with Allen, I'd let my kids go hungry, forego World Peace, and renounce chocolate for life.[22]

Whatever faults he had, Allen was a world-class kisser, with an expert thrusting of his tongue against mine. His mouth tasted fruity and slightly bitter at the same time, a good taste. The last lingering resistance melted away in that moment, and I found myself happy to be there. Allen waltzed me out of the guest room and across the hall into his room, tonguing me more and more deeply. We fell onto his bed with a crash. Dimly, I thought, we're not that heavy, the bed must not be as solid as it looks. Back to business, feeling hotter and bolder with every passing second, reaching my hands inside Allen's shirt and sliding them down his chest, still well-defined at seventy-five. As Allen in turn slid his hand inside my blouse, I heard moaning. I was getting there, fast track for sure, but it didn't sound like me. It didn't much sound like

---

21 No disrespect to my super-duper neon pink Bombex vibrator. Boldly advertised as your "Trusted Life Partner," it came pretty damn close to meeting that promise when lovers were in short supply. It may not have rubbed my shoulders or said a kind word, but when the chips are down that's what a massage therapist is for.

22 Milk chocolate, not the dark, let's be real.

Allen either. A few seconds later, assaulted by another loud crash and a sound that could not be mistaken for a moan, I almost levitated. Jesus, what was that! Yanked out of the trance we'd enjoyed seconds before, we went flying back through the narrow hallway toward the den, Allen leading the way.

What words could describe my immediate reaction to the vision that greeted us in Allen's den?

"Brought me up short?"

"Stopped me in my tracks?"

"Froze me in place?"

"Rendered me dumb?"

Those words are inadequate to address the spectacle I saw. Apparently, Allen wasn't the only resident of the manor who wanted to get lucky that afternoon, and the other guy hadn't wasted any time making his desires known. Knocking over a table in his eagerness to score—that was one of the crashes we heard—Allen's enormous Rottweiler had backed my sweet Hazel into a corner and attempted to mount her. He hadn't gotten all the way there, but with Hazel's hindquarters gripped firmly between his front legs, he was pumping away furiously. The big guy clearly had not encountered the surgeon's knife, proudly displaying a pair of testicles you could have played football with. And his shaft? Ye gods, it looked like one of those sausages you see hanging in the old delicatessens in New York, the ones that still sell the good pastrami.[23] Cyrus—that was the dog's noble name—ignored us and continued humping away vigorously, clearly enjoying this new damsel on whom he was (almost) succeeding in bestowing his considerable charms. Hazel, not so much. She was always a fastidious dog, so the mere fact that her neck was lathered with slobber would have been distasteful to her. Factor in that she had been spayed as a puppy and never been so much as approached by a male dog. Top it off with her age—she was then approaching her thirteenth year—and the slight arthritis she had developed in her hips, and you've got a pretty good idea of Hazel's state of mind. She wasn't enjoying this at all. To the contrary, she was somewhere between terrified and royally pissed. She was panting, clearly not from pleasure, and all the while continued to emit the noise that had ripped Allen and me away from our own embraces, a sound halfway between a whine and a howl that came from a place deep in her throat.

I leapt over a chair that was lying on its side—another casualty of Cyrus's ardor—and attempted to pry the dogs apart, all the while cooing "What a good dog, Hazel is such a good dog, it's all going to be fine, we're going to get that beast off of you in a jiffy, just you wait and see, such a good girl" and any other soothing utterances I could

---

23   Check out Katz's Delicatessen on E. Houston Street on the Lower East Side of Manhattan. That pastrami will make a convert out of you. On that note, a moment of silence please for Carnegie Deli, one more fallen giant. There aren't many places you can get a sandwich that weighs in at a pound these days.

think of. Allen leaned against the doorframe, seemingly unperturbed.

"Allen, what are you doing? Why aren't you helping me?"

"What's wrong?"

"What's wrong? Are you kidding me? My dog is collapsing under the weight of that elephant! She's old and she can't take this! Help me get him off her!"

Allen, still not moving, replied, "Hey, it's just nature taking its course, I say. Have at it!"

That's when I lost it. "Can you not see that my dog is hurting? Damn it, Allen, get over here and help me! I can't get him off by myself!"

Allen ambled over and gave a half-hearted tug at Cyrus's collar. Cyrus didn't budge. I grabbed the other side and we both gave his collar a solid yank. Progress. There were now about four inches of space between Cyrus's front legs and Hazel's hindquarters. Another yank, this one with as much force as I could muster on my side, and we separated the two dogs entirely. I landed on my ass on the scummy carpet and sat for a minute, catching my breath. Cyrus continued to pump away like a racing machine, undeterred by the lack of proximity of his quarry. Hazel didn't budge, seemingly paralyzed by the whole experience, but you could see in her eyes that she was relieved to be out of Cyrus's clutches.

As my composure began to return, the state of the carpet overwhelmed me—sticky, smelly, and altogether disgusting. I catapulted to my feet as if propelled by a trampoline and ran toward Hazel to reassure myself that she was okay. Allen intercepted me, took my arm and steered me in the other direction, to a two-seater sofa that sat in lonely splendor against the wall to the kitchen. Plopping down next to him, slightly dazed by the events of the last few minutes, I supposed that everything was okay, as long as Hazel was in no imminent danger. Granted, Cyrus continued to air hump my dog. Not for ten minutes. Not for twenty minutes. For the next forty-five minutes, I sat on that sofa and watched Cyrus engage in a masterpiece of simulated humping. He kept a respectful distance throughout the enterprise, and Hazel bore her trauma with the stoicism of the shelter dog that she had been for the first six months of her life.

Relaxing, I wondered what else could happen. Surely the universe had heaped enough on me for one day. Everything had to be easy going from here, right?

CHAPTER FIVE

—❦—

Dinner Is Served

At close to seven o'clock, hunger pangs struck. Breakfast was a distant memory and a skipped lunch made it impossible to ignore dinnertime.

"Allen, are you hungry yet?"

"Sure, I'll go grab the food."

"I'll help you."

"No, no you sit there; it won't take a minute."

True to his word, it didn't take Allen a minute. That's all the time it took to walk into the adjacent kitchen, pick up two Zaxby's boxes with plastic silverware and napkins taped to the top, and walk back into the den. Those boxes surely had not graced the inside of a refrigerator since my arrival. Who knew when the food had been picked up and how long it had sat out? Then there was the box itself. Eating dinner out of a Zaxby's box with plastic silverware was nowhere in my daydreams of how this encounter was going to go. How about a plate? A real fork and knife?

This was turning out to be quite the day for decisions. Stay? Go? Stick to just being "friends" with Allen? Have sex? Eat? Starve? Plastic? Stainless? Making a fuss about the dubious FDA rating of the salads was pretty low on the totem pole, at least compared to the other decisions I'd been called on to make so far, so I bit my tongue and accepted the box. Ripping open the bag that held the sad little fork and knife, I looked around for a place to set my dinner. Take that back—my knife was a casualty of the athleticism with which I opened the bag, and now lay in two pieces on my lap. The fork would have to do. Allen pulled over a "hospital tray table"—right down to the fake wood-grain laminate—and lowered it to dinner table level. Picking up the near-weightless fork to dig into the tepid salad, the room itself seemed to reflect the vibe that there was no "there" there.

To the right was an alcove that presumably had been designed as the dining room, but instead of a table in the middle, a massive wooden desk heaped with books and papers filled the space. From the floor to halfway up to the ceiling, stacks of brown accordion folders and manila files climbed, not only flush against the wall but also spreading out, so that there were only two narrow paths to and from the desk. Yellow legal pads with scribbles of blue ink lay scattered about. Faded green grass cloth covered the walls, much of which looked shredded by the family cat—unseen to this point—complimented by mismatched plaid curtains. Oh yeah, what about the missing cat? Had Cyrus stuffed its poor little body somewhere in a closet? I wouldn't put it past him? Psychopath.

Though the kitchen looked crammed, the dining room/office screamed "hoarder."

As one who is not a neatnik, never has been, even extreme disorder does not trouble me. People are constantly apologizing to me for the state of disarray in their homes, to which my honest response is that I don't even notice it, because I don't.

The mess in this house, on the other hand, was something that couldn't be ignored. The mountains of overflowing files and paperwork were overwhelming. Perhaps turning my head the other way would provide a more palatable view. Yikes, how wrong can a person be? To the left, a French door opened wide, leading out to what at first looked to be a room, but on further inspection took shape as a space comprised of a dirt floor enclosed by a large tarp on two sides. Covered by a piece of canvas that hung raggedly from a tall stick used to prop it up, the space actually served as the toilet for the dogs, from the look of the desiccated turds on the floor. Some, clearly attributable to Cyrus, were the size of hand grenades.[24]

---

24 More than one friend to whom I have related this tale stopped me at this exact point to question the verisimilitude of the story. To which I have responded uniformly, "You can't make this shit up."

That explained the smell. An odor had been vaguely noticeable in the den a few moments before, just doggy smell, right? After all, it takes a lot to maintain three dogs—two and a half if you want to be technical about the pitiful little greyhound—and while I don't love the smell of unwashed dogs, it wasn't the worst thing in the world. A serious horseback rider as a teenager, often mucking out the stalls as part of the tutelage, pungent animal smells are no more bothersome to me than the smell from a burning candle might be to others.

Besides, when it comes to food I'm not easily put off, generally able to overlook most anything that stands between a meal and me. Who cares what the kitchen in the back of the Chinese hole-in-the-wall restaurant looks like? Who cares if the cook used the hand sanitizer for twenty—not thirty—seconds before leaving the bathroom?

If the power went out from a hurricane raging outside, just bring on the vittles. If tom yum soup served in shacks in Thailand and oysters on the street in Istanbul hadn't put me off, nothing would.

Except…The smell in Allen's den seemed to grow more odiferous by the moment. As a result, not one morsel of that warm, wilted Zaxby's salad with the sharp smell of vinaigrette dressing, mixed with l'aire du dried dog poop, went in my mouth. Enough is enough. This was over the limit even for me. Putting down the plastic fork, I smiled at Allen and said, "You know what, I'm not hungry after all. I have a little bit of a stomach ache."

That was a lie, big time. Laying the groundwork for an early night, solo, perhaps even an early departure. Just as surely as Allen had been the be all and end all of mankind a few hours earlier, sent by a benevolent universe to take his place forevermore at my side, I now knew that he was a sad sack who was never, *ever* going to get any part of his anatomy near my tender parts, not ever. The power breakers in my head that flip off when the circuit shorts, well, they flipped off, and that's all she wrote. Hell hath no fury like a woman whose knight in shining armor fantasy has just been busted, and the remnants of mine lay in tatters all around, most particularly in the blighted "patio" to my left.

There was also a visual element to the repugnance now suffusing my feelings for Allen. A lifelong habit of reimagining, really re-"imaging," anyone I truly cared for was a nifty trick of mine. No matter how someone deviated from my interpretation of physical beauty when I first met them, it was all subject to re-imaging. Once I loved them, each one was magnificent, flawlessly beautiful, in my eyes. No matter how much time passed, their features would morph before me in real time. In the case of my now over-fifty friends, bumps, lumps, guts, thinning hair, gray hair, no hair, jowls, and all manner of fashion taboos magically transformed into images worthy of the runway.

In Allen's case, this process happened in reverse and at warp speed. Where only moments before he had appeared an attractively stocky man with endearingly crooked front teeth, his salt and pepper stubble sexy, and

43

yes, the most wonderful eyebrows, all bushy and manly; now he looked to me like an aging hippie in desperate need of a dentist, a shave, and an eyebrow trimmer, in that order.

Yuck.

In response to my prevarication that my stomach was hurting, Allen genially replied, "Oh that's too bad, sweetie. Pass your salad over and I'll eat it."

"Sure thing, here you go."

As I passed the Zaxby's container over to Allen, a furry arm batted at my hand, causing my grip to loosen and nearly spill wilted lettuce and lumpy vinaigrette dressing to the floor. Faster than I could follow, a tail disappeared under the sofa.

Regaining my grip on the container, I exclaimed, "Holy shit! That scared me! What *was* that?"

"That's Fonzi, my cat. He only comes out to eat or steal food."

Wow, just thinking about the cat, and then, like magic, there he appeared. Smart little dude, too, living under the sofa. Why take any chances with Cyrus around? The Rottweiler may not have killed the cat, but who knew what perversions that athlete was into? God knows Hazel would never be the same. Probably, she'd have to go to a doggy psychiatrist. Put her on Valium at any rate.

Resuming the handoff to Allen, he took the food container with one hand, groping for the television remote control with the other.

"Do you like to watch TV while you eat?"

Actually, yes, dining in front of the television is one of my favorite pastimes and surely time would pass more quickly that way as well. "Yeah, love to, what do you want to watch? Do you have cable? Are you a *Game of Thrones* fan? I need to catch up on the last season."

"No, I'm a news junkie, I don't watch much else."

Okay, a little educational TV couldn't hurt, certainly couldn't be worse than having to pretend that I was still into Allen.

On went Fox News. *Really?* Allen was Jewish, and the Jewish people I know don't watch Fox TV, that's an oxymoron. What rabbit hole was this? I looked around for a Red Queen or a tea party, but no, nothing of the sort appeared. Had Allen drugged me? Was this a test of some kind? A joke? Was someone hiding behind the bilious dining room cum office cum junk room cum hoarders' paradise curtains filming my reactions, waiting to spring out and trumpet, "Smile! You're on Candid Camera?"[25]

None of the above. Instead, we settled in to watch Allen's news channel of choice, a new experience for little old quasi-liberal independent *moi*. To my surprise, who was being interviewed but an old "friend," an ecclesiastical dignitary of the evangelical persuasion. We're talking fundamentalist, Bible-thumping evangelical. Not really

---

25 Candid Camera was a long-running television show in which unsuspecting souls were filmed in comedic situations without their knowledge and then discomfited by the cameraman jumping out of hiding, shouting "Surprise, You're on Candid Camera!" With the advent of cell phones, the practice became ubiquitous, popularly called "getting pranked." Obsolescence in action.

a friend, but someone I knew slightly through mutual friends, and whose daughter, Beverly, though younger than I, was a "twice-a-year-lady's-lunch" kind of acquaintance. Seeing her father's face on the television screen, a particularly memorable encounter surfaced. Beverly, a lovely person who lived in a very large, very gracious home, had invited me, along with eight of her better friends, to her house to join in the preparations for a high roller charitable function she was hosting. The local contemporary art museum was the beneficiary of the event, a worthy cause that I was happy to support.

We all came in casual clothes, planning to change later into our formal gowns. After working all day putting together massive flower arrangements and silent auction tables full of local wares and gift certificates, not to mention arranging custom Matisse-printed hand towels in the "his" and "hers" powder rooms, we all convened in an upstairs bedroom to change into our formal attire. As I pulled on my brand new, style-of-the-hour, elegant-as-could-be dress, the zipper got stuck all the way down at the bottom—can you say "crack of my ass?"—and no amount of tugging, pulling, or pushing could make it budge. Without hesitation Beverly, clearly her father's daughter, pulled me and the other women into a small circle and invited us to pray over the zipper.

This was a new one on me, but I tried not to show my ignorance of a tactic obviously well known to the others. Taking my cue from them, I mumbled The Lord's Prayer, while the other ladies, clearly in the zone, went at it with zest. To the best of my recollection, their prayer went something like, "Heavenly Father, please have mercy on this dress and in your omnipotence and boundless compassion repair the zipper which has failed her so that Lynn might be restored to her rightful state of happiness and harmony. In Jesus' name we pray, Amen."

The prayers didn't work—some candle wax liberally applied to the zipper fortunately did—but the moment was classic.

CHAPTER SIX

A Silverfish by Any Other Name

Seeing Beverly's father on TV felt a bit nostalgic, which was a nice counterbalance to the antipathy that Allen had begun to inspire in me. Demonstrating an impressive lack of insight, Allen chose that exact moment to pick up where we had left off before our canine intervention, laying a heavy hand way up high on my thigh. His hand was red and his fingers slightly curled, and sitting on my leg it reminded me of a crab stranded on the beach. No longer "in the mood" was an epic understatement.

"Allen, it's really hot in here and my stomach still hurts. Do you mind scooting over and giving me a little space?"

Allen put on a hurt puppy look, like someone had taken away his favorite bone. He removed his hand and shifted his bulk a millimeter to the side. In his favor, there wasn't much space on the two-seat sofa.

Nevertheless, my annoyance level escalated. "Hey, really, I'm burning up here (not really). Tell you what, I'll go sit on the chair."

The only other piece of furniture in the room was a straight-backed wooden chair, upholstery nonexistent. Within seconds of sitting on it, my backside started hurting. That's how hard it was. My temper did not improve.

Starting to get the picture, Allen said: "What's going on? I feel like you are disconnecting from me."

He didn't quite get it right. Unhinging, unhooking, uncoupling, and getting ready to be effing gone was more like it.

"Allen, I came here to get to know you as a friend and I guess I feel like that's not really happening."

In my experience, nothing pisses a guy off like playing the friend card when sex is already on the table. That doesn't change from grammar school to the grave, and I played that card like Omar Sharif[26] playing to win the World Bridge Championship. Most guys would have reacted with annoyance at least, but Allen showed none, instead picking up the gauntlet with seeming nonchalance: "Okay, what do you want to know?"

Right, two could play the friend game.

---

26 Talk about a looker. At present ineligible by reason of being dead.

I asked: "Tell me about your relationships since you were married? Have you dated out a lot? Had any long-term relationships?"[27]

Looking thoughtful, Allen reached across the space between us, picked up my leg and put it into his lap. Crap. After all this he puts my leg in his lap? Clearly, he was still on the chase. Was this never going to end? What did I need to do for this guy to get the message?

As it turned out, I had to do just one thing. As he talked about himself, he unwittingly provided me the clue to ending this game.

"My relationships? Oh sure, I've dated a lot," he said. "After all, my wife died twelve years ago. It took a while, but I finally got back into the dating scene."

Me, on the offensive: "Anything long term? How long was your longest relationship?"

---

27   Single men and women alike hate those questions. If you have been single for more than a year there is no right answer; anything you say makes you look like a loser. Don't believe me? Consider scenario number one, in which the person answers, "I had three relationships that lasted more than six months in the last five years. I was really in love, but they just didn't work out." Everyone thinks, "What's wrong with him/her—can't commit? Significant other finally ditched them? There must be a problem. Loser!"

Now consider scenario number two, in which the answer is: "I've had loads of dates in the last three years, but no long-term relationships. I never could find anyone I liked well enough to go out with for longer than a month." Now everyone thinks, "Uh-oh, this one's living in fantasy land, expects to find the perfect person. Umpty ump years old and still hasn't figured it out. Loser!"

And scenario number three? "I've gone on lots of dating websites, but I never get picked. I've only had three dates in the last two years. I can't figure it out." And we all say together, "Loser!"

"I had two long-term relationships. One was a year and a half and the other three years. But in the end they didn't work out."

"What happened?"

"They both wanted to change me. They complained about my house, the way I lived, the way I dressed. At first things were great, and then all of a sudden it seemed like they were complaining about everything. They kept telling me to move this or get rid of that or wear something different. They even wanted me to get rid of my dogs! They were both quality ladies and I really cared about them, but I got sick of them trying to change me. With me, what you see is what you get."

No kidding. I knew what I had to do. "Amigo," I thought, "didn't you ever hear 'don't look a gift horse in the mouth?'" He should have grabbed one of those ladies and hauled them to the altar posthaste. They must have been (a) saints, (b) desperate, (c) flat busted broke, (d) extremely horny, or (e) all of the above.

What I said, though, was, "Allen, geez, sorta weird telling you this, but I've been accused of being the same way (never happened). Guys have said it drives them crazy the way I am easygoing at first, then turn into a drill sergeant who wants to make them change (nope, not me). Don't you think it's nice when someone tries to change things for the better? (Hate this, wouldn't dream of it.)"

Allen, with a fair amount of heat, "No, I don't! I'm seventy-five years old and I am very comfortable with who I am and how I live."

Time to feint. "What about the mess, the papers piled to the ceiling, the smell of dog poop? You may like how you live, but wouldn't it be better if I got things all cleaned up and organized for you?" Deftly inserting the pronoun "I" to really freak him out.

Allen jumped right on it: "Did you just say 'I'? What do you mean, 'I'?"

Bingo. Time to parry. Adopting a conciliatory, "Did I say that? I didn't mean it. I would never try to change you. I have too much respect for you. Don't you know that?" This was a delicate balancing act. On one hand, my goal was to eighty-six any possibility of amorous pursuit by Allen. On the other hand, it was important to return us as gracefully as possible to our status as business colleagues, since Allen would continue to be a significant presence in my professional life.

"Okay, sure, I guess so," Allen muttered, at the same time moving my leg off his lap and standing up. "I need to use the facilities. Be right back."

"Okay, I'll take Hazel out; she probably has to go."

Nicely done. If I didn't miss my guess, his needle was about to come to rest somewhere between a little affronted and somewhat mollified. Ideally with the steam of sex evaporated like a Starbucks latte left too long at the counter. Perfect.

"Hazel, come on, let's go out."

She stood up and stretched, no worse for the wear it appeared. Maybe no Valium after all; just a little Xanax. Lucky for her, her trials seemed to be over. The vigor of

Cyrus's humping apparently had served to slake his pro-digious sexual thirst, leaving him curled up in a corner, snoring contentedly. Pocketing my phone, I put on Hazel's leash and walked her out the kitchen door. The front yard, which was around the corner from the driveway where I'd parked, seemed the safest bet from a sanitary standpoint, and so it was. Nice and clean, and there was a light breeze blowing. There were even a few bushes, half-heartedly trying to hang on to the gritty red clay soil, flanked by a gravel path, its pebbles orange-hued from the ubiquitous clay. My equanimity, and more bracing, my sense of out-rage, began to return. What did I owe Allen? Why was I trying to smooth the waters by staying?

There's nothing like a friend in times of crisis, so I called my girlfriend, Nancy. She had suffered through my mooncalf ramblings about Allen every step of the way for the last several months.

"Oh my God," Nancy shrieked, "Is it great? Are you in love? Why aren't you in bed screwing your brains out?"

"Nancy, this is a no go like you can't believe. A com-plete bust."

"What? Tell me everything!"

"Later. But tell me quick while Allen's in the bathroom whether you can think of any reason I can give for not staying the night."

"Wow, okay," she said. "Give me a minute. I don't know, pretend like you're sick?"

"Yeah, already tried that, but what about a reason to bolt right now? Gimme something better than that."

"Lynn?" Allen's voice carried through the screen door to the kitchen. "Hey where are you?"

"Nancy, got to go. I'll call you back later."

Cutting her off, I pulled Hazel out of the bush she was inspecting and replied, "Out here, I'll be right in."

Finding the kitchen empty, I continued into the den. There sat Allen, reclining in his spot on the pint-sized sofa. He looked up and announced, nonchalantly: "Know what? I have to get up early tomorrow to visit my mother, so I'm going to go to bed."

"Huh?" I thought. He's going to bed at 8:00 p.m.? I thought I was supposed to be the one doing the ditching here. What was I supposed to do the rest of the night?

Allen had that one figured out. He patted the sofa next to him and said, "Sit here and watch TV 'til you're ready to go to bed. Here's the remote."

On autopilot, I smiled sweetly and said, "Sure, I'll see you in the morning."

As Allen handed the remote to me, he stood up. I sat down, too overwhelmed to process one more thing. The day's events had finally caught up with me, and a state of laissez-faire set in. I had no more fight left, no more Machiavellian strategies to concoct. All that was left was the core of my very Southern upbringing: don't cause a scene. There is a limit to the utility of good manners, an excellent lesson to learn for another day, but at the moment my upbringing took over. I Yam what I Yam.[28]

---

28 Those who know it hum along, "I'm Popeye the sailor man. I live in a garbage can...." Ah, for simpler times.

Allen walked over to the wall next to his "office" and started turning lights off, until it was nearly dark in the den. I hate sitting in the dark, but I kept quiet.

"See over here?" Allen said, indicating a spot on the wall next to the wheezing refrigerator. "That's the last switch in this room to turn off when you're done. Then go in the kitchen and turn off this switch."

"Okay, I'll take care of it."

"See you in the morning. Sleep well." With a wave of his hand, Allen disappeared down the hall to his bedroom, Cyrus padding heavily behind him. At least things had turned around for Hazel.

As for me, paralyzed, sitting on the dingy sofa, the remote in my right hand and the leash in my left, I looked down at Hazel.

"Good girl," I said, unsnapping her leash, "Lie down over there and we'll be out of here in the morning. Go relax now that Cyrus the Golgothan[29] is gone."

The TV was still tuned to Fox News. With no idea how to work the remote and fetching Allen out of the question, I couldn't change the channel. My grasp of technology is reasonable for an aging baby boomer, but remote controls strike terror deep in my heart. There are so many buttons and the writing so cryptic. What does "Aux" mean? "EPG?" For all I knew, I could screw up Allen's settings with the touch of a button. Why that worried me,

---

29   I learned of the dung monster called "Golgathan," who saps the will of its victims with the overpowering smell of its excrement, from one of my favorite movies, *Dogma*. From what I could tell, Cyrus had him beat.

considering Allen's lack of hospitality—and his home's lack of habitability—is a mystery, but at the time it seemed like a terrifying prospect. Frozen in place, I watched the screen as something called *Stossel* came on.

There is a God.

Stossel turned out to be a lively roundtable discussion of topics such as civil liberties and health care seen from opposing viewpoints. The moderator, John Stossel, took the libertarian point of view, and all in all, it made for interesting viewing.

As time passed, I no longer felt overwhelmed and even started to unwind. I hardly noticed when one of Allen's dogs, the unattractive terrier—inaccurately named Bella—jumped in my lap. Nudging her to the other seat on the sofa I absently petted her head. Until I noticed that she was nonstop scratching herself. Shooing the dog off the sofa, I looked at the clock. It was already 10:00 p.m.! Still early, but not an unreasonable time to go to bed.

With slight trepidation, I attempted to turn the television off. Success! There, not such a tech moron after all. "Come on Hazel, up!" Following Allen's instructions, I turned off all of the lights. With Hazel at my heels, my phone's flashlight guided us down the hall into my bedroom. Opening my suitcase, I extracted a nightgown, put it on and crossed the hall to the bathroom. "Hello, sleeping pills," I said, downing an extra half pill for good measure. When I travel the uneven quality of my sleep sometimes requires pharmacological assistance, so my meds had come along as a matter of course. Using them after my chaotic evening with Allen was a no brainer.

Returning to the bedroom, a surprise waited on my pillow. None other than Bella, scratching away. Shouting "Move! Get off! Get Down! Now!" I swiped at the dog with my hand. She jumped off the bed and exited the room while I stood stock still. Had my shout wakened Allen? No, all remained quiet. Suddenly the bed looked a whole lot less inviting. Was this a frequent napping spot for Bella? Were there fleas on my pillow? Inside the sheets?

Tiptoeing over, I scrutinized the pillow. So far so good. At least there were no visible signs of fleas, and a towel over the pillow could serve as an additional precaution.

Next, the bed itself. Gingerly, I pulled back the comforter, though fairly certain that, based on the clean pillow and the general tidiness of the room, everything would be fine.

Gah! Ergh! Eek! Ergh again! Gah again! Klaxons! Alarms! SOS! May Day! May Day! Batten down the hatches! Call in the Marines!

Surely my eyes deceived me. Could that be flea excrement there? And there. And there. Could that be a silverfish skittering across the sheets?[30] Yes? No? What? What? All of my systems were blowing at once, vertigo taking over. Okay, gotta think, gotta think. Though I barely knew what a silverfish looked like, I was pretty sure I had just seen one live and in the flesh (or carapace, as the case may

---

30 Embellishment on my part, you're sure of it. Nope, not a syllable.

be). Flinging the covers back up to the top of the bed, I stood rooted in place, breathing hard. What to do? Wake Allen? Then what? Sleep in his bed? Oh hell no. If the choice was either the end of the world or me sleeping in this bed, it was going to be "so long world, nice knowing you."

Heart still palpitating, the lawyer in me took over. Forget where to sleep; suddenly it seemed paramount to get a picture of that silverfish. If Allen thought I was lying, proof of the silverfish's existence would take care of that.

Have I implied that I was lucid at this moment? That's what I thought. Don't criticize.

Grabbing my phone from the dresser, I set it on video and steeled myself to rip the cover back again and catch that sucker on film. Lights camera, action. Okay little buddy, gotcha. No, you can't get away by burrowing further under the covers; we'll just peel them back more. No matter if you have about a billion legs, you can't move fast enough. There is no escape.

Mission accomplished, the video saved and stored,[31] then sent to my email for good measure. For some reason I took comfort in having multiple copies of this critical piece of evidence. Maybe I could sue Allen for intentional infliction of emotional distress. Even as a non-litigator, I know that's extremely hard to prove, but in this instance it seemed like a slam dunk. A freaking silverfish in my bed? Your Honor, I rest my case.

---

31 Not kidding. Saved for posterity and available for your viewing pleasure at www.lynngarson.com/silverfish

Documentary complete, it was time to think about my own escape, if I could keep my eyes open while planning it. Now that the adrenaline had worn off, the sleeping pills were starting to kick in. Dear Lord, if this was to be my version of Theseus escaping the Labyrinth, could a sister at least get some help?

CHAPTER SEVEN

The Great Escape

What to do? What else but call Nancy.

"Nancy, are you there? Goddamn it, pick up, come on, *pick up!*"

Waking with a start, Hazel looked up in alarm, disturbed by the hissing sound of my efforts not to wake Allen. Until that moment she had been curled up on the floor, twitching, and from time to time, growling softly in her dreams. Probably reliving those awful moments of siege by Cyrus and his outsized member.[32]

---

32 My years of immersion in crappy romance novels included some that tilted the scale ever so slightly on the side of porn. (Does the title *Fanny Hill* ring a bell with anyone?) They always called penises "members" in those books. I used to wonder why. Did penises belong to their own club? Was it an early, more genteel expression of the tendency men have to personalize their dicks? (Dick, Johnson, Peter; you get my drift.) I use the word "member" now with a certain nostalgia. Oh for the days when porn was at once innocent and exciting.

"Quiet, girl, help is on the way." If only it were true.

Yes! After a few more rings, miraculously Nancy's voice came on the line: "Lynn, hey, glad you could call back. Is Allen…"

I cut her off, "Listen, Nancy, you gotta help, I just went to…"

"What? I can't hear you. Why are you whispering like that?"

"Goddamn it, I can't talk any louder!" My sibilant whispers sounded like a tea kettle sitting on high too long. "Turn up your volume or something! Fix the sound! Can you hear me now?"

She clicked the volume on her phone higher, but it took what seemed like eternity, though it was only a few seconds until she replied, "Yes, okay, I can hear you! Lynn, what on earth is going on?"

"A minute ago, in bed, I mean, the bed in the guest room, it looked fine, it really did, but beneath the covers this horrible bug was running around on the sheet. Disgusting. Gigantic. And there was flea crap, too. Everywhere. You wouldn't believe it, it was so awful. What should I do?"

Thankfully, my friends are usually smarter and more collected in an emergency than I am. In her most soothing voice, Nancy said, "Okay, calm down, you're fine. This is easy, no choice, really. Grab your stuff and haul ass out of there right now. Got it?"

"Okay, got it. You're right, of course. Okay. Yeah. Let me get everything together. Keep your phone on 'cause I'm gonna need your help."

For once, it was a simple matter to get everything back into my suitcase, and before you could say "one, two, three," I should have been headed out the door. If not for the fact that, inexplicably, the compulsion to leave Allen a note was overwhelming. Don't say it. Just don't. At least let me try to explain the inexplicable. Huddled in a basement awaiting the end of the world, polite exchanges would still be mandatory:

Achoo!

God Bless You!

Thank you!

You're welcome!

Thank you, that's very nice!

No, really, you're welcome!

Are you sure you're okay?

Oh yes, just a bit of a cold. I guess the bombs will take care of that!

Get it?

A notepad and pen conveniently lay on the bedside table. If only Mr. Silverfish or one of his buddies would not get me first. Under the covers or not, an invertebrate surviving since the dawn of time and infesting people's bed sheets at will is an animal to be feared.

Searching for the right words was fruitless, so I settled for, "Sorry I had to leave. Horrible bugs were in my bed. I even have a video of them. Thanks for inviting me." Despite all that had transpired, the word "silverfish" still wouldn't come. It was just too embarrassing and I didn't want to hurt his feelings *that* badly.

That wouldn't be good manners.

Growing up in the South is a bitch.

Leaving the note on the dresser, I grabbed my suitcase with one hand, snatched up Hazel's leash with the other. "Get up, girl, we are outta here," I whispered. She popped up like a jack in the box, eager to go someplace free of sexual predators like Cyrus. A peek out of the door revealed a dark hallway, lit only by slivers of moonlight filtering through cracks in the tarp. We tiptoed slowly down the hall, accompanied by a sound I couldn't place, a sound that went "creak, creak...." What was that? Oh right, that suitcase makes noise when it rolls. Fine, no problem. I picked it up, holding the bag with nine fingers, the tenth hooked around Hazel's leash.

Damn, the suitcase was heavy. What had possessed me to bring four pairs of shoes for two days? "God, I promise I will do more upper body work if you get me out of here. No more two-pound weights, I'll go for the five, I swear it, on my honor."

Or was it the sleeping pills that were making not only the suitcase, but my arms and legs, too, feel so heavy, like moving against a current?

Speeding up, from the hallway into the den, The Almighty must have been listening, because so far I'd made it undiscovered.

Ruff! Ruff! Ruff, ruff, ruff!

What on earth was that? Oh no! That flea-ridden hag, Bella, was barking her head off. The dog had caught wind of my skedaddle and was trying her level best to alert her master. Just what I needed, the latter-day spawn of Cerberus.

"Shhh, shhh, shut up, quiet, good doggy, nice girl," I whispered, staggering past the dog with my suitcase.

Hazel whimpered slightly, her neck cocked at an odd angle and her body turned sideways due to the pressure of the suitcase on my arms. Leaning towards Bella and cooing soothingly, "That's a good girl, yes you're a sweetie, what a nice dog," somehow worked. She quieted, miraculously. Just a few more steps to the kitchen, then on to the screen door.

Out the door, we made it to my car. Hurling Hazel in, followed by the suitcase, I quietly closed the back door. Then, lunacy struck. Did I leave the note for Allen on the dresser? Uh, maybe not. Did I? Can't remember. Gotta make sure it's there. Gotta go back and check.

In the cold light of day, after the fact, there is no explanation for this. None. It may be the single stupidest thought I've ever had. Blame it on adrenaline, sleep meds, temporary insanity, or a mixture of all three. Whatever the reason, going back inside seemed like a good idea at the time.

Back to the screen door. Back through the kitchen. Back into the hallway. At least this time my hands were free to use the flashlight on my phone. Halfway down the hallway, I randomly tilted the phone to the left. On the counter of the bathroom sink sat my entire makeup bag, overlooked in my haste to pack and get out of the house.

My sigh of relief was so loud I clapped my hand over my mouth, afraid to waken Bella and set her barking or worse yet, rouse Allen himself.

For men reading this,[33] instead of a makeup bag, imagine a gold watch passed down from your grandfather through your father to you, inscribed with a dedication from President Roosevelt for valor in service of our country. You might get the barest hint of what a makeup bag means to a woman.

"Thank you, God. I will add pushups to my regimen. A deal's a deal."

Retrieving the makeup bag, I turned into the guestroom, flipped the light on and yes, there was the note to Allen. Considering that my unreasoning adherence to etiquette only equals my dislike of confrontation, going back into Allen's house did not make any sense at all. For those who are puzzled, annoyed or downright pissed at me, I get it.

Back down the hallway, through the den, that canine gatekeeper of the underworld, Bella, was nowhere to be found. One final look into the patio in the moonlight revealed the walls festooned with birds' nest palaces and cobweb canyons. In the dim light, almost inviting. If I'd had a lobotomy.

Time to move again, out the screen door. Lock it? How? Too bad. If someone comes in and murders Allen

---

33 When I wrote *Sex and the Single Grandma*, I thought it was a chick book. Surprisingly, the men in my writers group and a few male friends who read the manuscript loved it. Perhaps what attracts them is the opportunity for a view behind curtains not often parted.

in his bed, it's not my fault. He should have thought of that before he stuck me in a room with a silverfish on steroids.

Finally, some gumption. I felt inordinately proud.

Back at the car, careful to close my door quietly, I debated. Turn on the engine? The lights? No, that might wake Allen. If they can do it in the movies, I can, too. Just put the car in neutral and let it roll backwards down the driveway slope. How hard can it be? Who needs headlights anyway?

Five minutes later, the car bumped over the curb at the foot of Allen's short, gently inclined driveway. Drenched in sweat,[34] known far and wide as the world's worst backer-upper, Allen's driveway had tested me mightily.

Still coasting, I applied the brakes, stopped and turned the ignition. It started! One final look at Allen's house, then I hit the gas and stared straight ahead until I turned off the street, wound back the same way I'd come through this godforsaken neighborhood. Zaxby's greeted me at the corner, which seemed only fitting. One thing for sure, they wouldn't get any of my business for the next decade or two. If you can't shoot the perpetrator, shoot the messenger.

A combination gas station and convenience store appeared at the next light, a perfect place to top off my tank and buy a soda. The attendant, a young man with hair coiffed in the tallest mullet on record, turned out to

---

34 At this stage of life, it takes either a ninety-minute hot yoga class or a life-threatening emergency to make me sweat. Thanks, Allen.

be a goldmine of information on nearby dog-friendly hotels. On second thought, however, staying anywhere near Allen's house gave me the willies. What if he got out early, drove by, and spotted my green Lexus? Maybe not terribly rational, but logic had long since abandoned ship, replaced by fear: fear of being on my own so late at night, fear of trying to drive while fighting the effects of sleeping pills, residual fear from the great escape, just plain fear. No, the risk of an encounter with Allen so soon, however improbable, was way too scary. Our law practices would probably require a meeting in a couple of weeks or a month, but as distasteful as that thought might be, at least by then my equilibrium should have returned.

Back to the car with a snack for trusty Hazel, I followed the signs to the highway leading back to Atlanta. Once I hit the on ramp, free and clear, I headed for home.

Home. So close and yet so far away. If only my eyelids would stop fluttering. After a few minutes more on the highway there was no ignoring the effects of the pills taken a mere forty-five minutes earlier, though it seemed a lifetime ago. Time to call Nancy.

"Hey, are you out of there?" Nancy inquired. She sounded sleepy, which was not surprising for someone whose habit was to retire before 10:00 p.m. most nights. It was now a few minutes before midnight.

"Yes, and I need your help. I took sleeping pills, and now I'm on the highway falling asleep, so I'm not going to make it home."

"Wow, this is turning into quite the adventure, isn't it? Okay, let me get on my laptop to find you a hotel."

"Remember, I've got Hazel, so they have to take dogs."

A rule breaker would have taken the first hotel she came to and snuck her dog in, but obedience to rules is second only to my adherence to good manners. If at this point you are incredulous, have a few more conversations with any women of your acquaintance who were raised in the Deep South in the 1950s.

"Where are you?"

"Wait a minute, I'm between exits. Okay here comes a sign. Exit 258." [35]

"Great, there are a few motels just ahead. Let me call."

After multiple conversations with night clerks to make sure I would be safe, Nancy—what a friend!—guided me to a Motel 6 fifteen minutes farther down the road. Exiting the highway with the last vestiges of wakefulness I could muster, I drove up to the motel, parked, got Hazel out and the two of us checked in. No elevator in sight, I climbed a flight of stairs with Hazel in tow, plus a little bag of clothes and toiletries from my suitcase. Walking into the room, then straight to the bathroom, I found a paper cup, filled it with water and set it on the floor for Hazel. Stripping, I pulled on a t-shirt and climbed into bed. The sheets were

---

35 Much as Allen is on my shit list I don't want to out him, so the exit number and anything else that could be used to identify him is changed just enough to foil any amateur detectives out there. So don't bother trying to triangulate Zaxby's locations with downtrodden neighborhoods and houses with weeping willows in the yard. It won't work.

thin and scratchy, that color of gray that is just noticeable enough to signify a fourth-rate lodging, but who cared? As long as they were free of fauna, it was all good. I fell asleep within seconds.

On nights after taking sleeping pills, I usually sleep like a log, and this was no exception. After nine blissful hours, light poured in through the blinds. I stretched and sat up. Where was I? Oh yes, somewhere in rural Georgia.

As usual, Hazel had slept on the bed. She was lying on her back, stomach pointed to the ceiling. After twelve years, that stomach and all of its markings were as familiar as the back of my hand. A little black spot looked out of place. Spying a second unfamiliar spot, and a third, a sense of dread crept over me. One word. Bella. Don't tell me. It can't be true.

Oh, yes it can!

Of course it was true. Hazel had fleas. My Hazel! Not just one or two, but an army of fleas. In bed. With me.

Naturally the itching started, even though logically there couldn't be many fleas on me, if any. Was that a red spot on my arm?

Throwing my clothes into the bag, I put Hazel on her leash and went down the stairs triple time. After a few seconds for Hazel to do her business in the grass next to the motel, she and the bag went into the car. Back on the highway, I put Siri[36] to work searching for the telephone number of the PetSmart nearest my home.

---

36   This was no time for dramatic persona changes, so I let Siri roll in her natural state, which sounded soothingly competent.

Praise be, they answered right away and made my day with an open appointment right about the time we would arrive in Atlanta. I floored the accelerator.

What to do on the long drive to distract myself? What else? Call Nancy to de-brief.

There is no substitute for a close girlfriend. None. Especially one who happens to be facing many of the same dating challenges at the same time. Many women, including me, have been guilty of ditching our girlfriends when "the guy" comes along. It has taken a measure of maturity for me to understand how little this serves me. And a willingness to be vulnerable enough to admit my own fear of being ditched the same way. Nancy is the kind of friend that I can tell, and have told, that I'm afraid that I will be left out in the cold when she is dating. It's understandable, and I would forgive it, but I don't like the prospect. She reassures me that she wouldn't do that, and I believe her. It's a great comfort to be able to talk about things like that. As well as the trials and tribulations of dating over fifty. I wouldn't trade a friend like that for anything in the world. Guys come and guys go, even husbands can come and go, but a true girlfriend is forever.

Talk we did. Mostly I complained and Nancy listened, inserting appropriately soothing noises every once in a while. A thirty-minute call is nothing for us, and this one extended long beyond. Finally, I wound down, a little calmer and less daunted by the task of ridding Hazel and my belongings of unwelcome guests. Conveniently close to my house, I signed off to continue the rest of the trip with Stevie Nicks on the radio as my companion.

Any dog owner knows the fire drill that followed my arrival at home. It is not dissimilar to the fate of Sisyphus[37] and equally taxing. Suffice it to say that the Scorched Earth Flea Prevention and Elimination Campaign that I mounted was successful and, unlike Sisyphus's task, did come to an end, and entailed minimal, though painful, casualties. Principal among them was Hazel's leash and collar and, sadly, also the beloved makeup bag that I rescued from Allen's bathroom. Talk about adding insult to injury.

During the days that followed, I fully expected Allen to call. With an apology, at the very least, after he recovered from my note. What's that, you say? Did you just call me an idiot? Right you are. My phone remained silent.

Several days went by with no word, then several more. My prodigious capacity for guilt began to weigh heavily, and I inquired of a couple of friends whether the error was mine. Did I owe Allen a call instead of vice versa? While varied in style, their answers had a certain uniformity:

"No."

"Hell, no!"

"I will break your arms if you call him. Then I'll break your legs."

"What is wrong with you? Are you out of your mind?"

---

37 In Greek mythology, Sisyphus was a king whose punishment it was to roll a huge boulder up a hill, and when it rolled back down, to do it again. And again. And again. Get the picture?

So, I didn't call Allen. Six months later, he finally called me to begin a contract negotiation between our clients. A few minutes into the call he offered a lame apology about not checking in sooner—something to do with a family member getting sick—but with no emotional investment one way or another, I listened politely (yep, that's me) and got off the phone as soon as possible. And never laid eyes on Allen again.

Hazel did, however, accept a date from Cyrus.

Just kidding.

 INTERLUDE

Selected JDate messages sent to the author:

Message #1

MAN: *Hi nice to hear from you. I have been on the site for a while and been single over 7 years. I joined the site looking for my soulmate and have not had any luck so far. What do you do for fun? what is your favorite color? what type of relationship are you looking for? I look forward to your reply.*

As a Spanish friend once famously said, "No es mi tipo." A little too needy.

Message #2

MAN: *I guess pressing the orange icon gets you a flirt. Anyway, I read your page and it looks like you had an interesting life. We seem to have a lot in common (even one of my sons spent a semester at Hong Kong University of Science and Technology). I have been to Hong Kong as part of a People-to People Ambassador program. To be totally honest, my life is in limbo. I am recovering from recent open heart surgery but doing well. I am the type that does laps around the Nurses Station, but I am trying to slow down and follow instructions. I am however, back to work and driving short distances. Also, I thought my girlfriend of 4 years had let me go, I then joined J Date but then she texted me that she could talk to me at an undetermined time in the future. So my life is kind of on hold until I can get things sorted out and fully recover. Anyway, Nice job on your profile.*

This guy seemed like a real person, and I felt badly for him, so I replied:

LYNN: *Good luck with your recovery and with the girlfriend. A word of TOTALLY unsolicited advice, but you seem like a nice guy. It seems like your girlfriend has the upper hand in a big way. Unless you did something reprehensible (and maybe even if you did), you might want to consider taking a little control back. Otherwise IMHO things get unbalanced—I've been there and it hasn't felt good. Anyway, good luck.*

We had a couple more amiable exchanges and I counted that one a "win."

Messages #3, 4, 5, 6, 7, 8, 9 . . .

The following accounts for fully fifty percent of the messages I received after the initial flurry of positive responses on JDate:

This member's account has been removed for violating our terms of service. They may have been using a false identity and/or may pose a risk of attempting to obtain money from other members through fraudulent means. As a reminder, you should NEVER send money or personal financial information to another member of the site. For more information on how you can protect your online safety and avoid scam, click here.

Do I have a special talent for attracting these creeps or are they really that pervasive? Either way, get a life!

PART THREE

Peter

CHAPTER ONE

———— ♛ ————

Casual Sex, Anyone? Anyone?

In the aftermath of the visit with Allen, a grand romance as prelude to a long-term relationship had lost its appeal. Instead, a casual sexual encounter, a fling, seemed like just the ticket. No drama, no great expectations, just sex, plain and unadorned. Why not? The few minutes of sensuous foreplay at Allen's house had left me hungry for more. As a woman who had come of age during the peak of the sexual revolution, no-strings-attached sex did not trouble me, at least theoretically. In college, it was almost obligatory to sleep with a man after the third date[38]—before that you

---

38 When I told my writers group this, the men commented that when they were single, they had expected sex on the first date. They would have gotten along well with Cyrus.

were a slut and after that you were a prude—and while part of me continued to yearn for love and romance, another part of me became inured to sex that was, shall we say, somewhat less meaningful.

Thinking more about it, the idea grew on me. Hmm. Maybe? Yes. Yes! I would do it. To just have sex and walk away, yes I would. Time to pull out my old MacBook Air, settle into my red sofa—always comfy despite the slight sag in the cushions—and embark on this new adventure.

Having embraced the idea of a fling, it remained to find a willing partner. This may sound easy, and indeed it might be for any number of liberated women. Not for me. Terminally unsure of myself, the thought of the bar scene was overwhelming, as always. Distasteful memories from decades past came flooding back. Memories of forcing myself to preen and flirt in bars and pretend that it was fun. What did those terminally vivacious people find to shout about, above the din of the crowd? What was so terribly amusing that they all threw their heads back and laughed fit to bust? I still don't know. For a person like me who is attractive more in her openness, directness, honesty, and incisiveness than in the subtleties of flirting, the bar scene was a non-starter.

Fix-ups? Hardly. After the initial burst of dates generated by my friends, exactly one fix-up in all the years since my divorce was the sorry record. And that was by my mother's hairdresser. Oh, I forgot, there was one more, but he doesn't count because he turned out to be a wife-killer.

For real.[39] Anyway, my mother had abandoned the salon after a falling out, so the odds weren't good that her stylist, the debonair Mr. Donald, would be interested in playing Cupid again. For another thing, who would want to fix me up when all I wanted was a fling? Who would pimp me out? Nobody.

The easiest route, a no-brainer really, was to renew membership on a couple of internet dating sites, set the hook, sit back, and wait. The bait would be taken and there would be at least a few responses that skipped the preliminaries and went all the way to an invitation to bed. In the past, men who responded to me with overtly sexual comments merited an automatic delete. That wasn't the idea, oh no, how dare they stomp on a *noble quest for love*. Well this time was different. My new quest was the updated, twenty-first century, take-no-prisoners kind of quest that would lead to an exchange of bodily fluids and nothing more.

With Hazel by my side for moral support, answers to the profile questions that were a prerequisite to joining the dating sites came easily. Lines like "adventurous, sexy lady" and "sexy mama" made me gag, but were a necessary evil. As were a couple of sexy photos. Those were a little hard to

---

39 The full story is recounted in *Southern Vapors*, but in short, several years ago I went on a date with a man who, it turned out, had been investigated for killing his wife. The prosecutor had to drop the case because my date had had his wife's body cremated in Mexico the day she "died," thereby neatly eliminating any direct evidence. He had also been convicted and served time for Medicaid fraud. Coincidentally—or not, depending on your belief system—I found this all out because the guy's wife had been besties with the law partner for whom I was working at the time.

find, but with some judicious cropping of a couple of shots stored on my laptop, "sexy" was a fitting description.

After a couple of hours, legs cramped from being crossed in one position and fingers stiff from typing, the effort paid off. The job was done. After hitting "enter," I got up, stretched my legs and went for a snack. This being one of my healthier phases, the refrigerator greeted me with hummus, carrots, sprouted bread, guacamole, and berries. The pantry sported almonds and dried apple bits, rice crackers, and some kind of ancient date balls with a little dried coconut. Not a double-stuffed Oreo in sight. Oh well, almonds it was.

Wandering back to the sofa, my computer dinged with one message alert followed closely by a second. The web masters[40] on both dating sites had simultaneously responded that my photos would be reviewed and notification sent if they were acceptable, but otherwise my membership was live. A tense day followed while my shots went out; shots that make or break a woman's success in the online dating world, at least in America. Maybe in the court of the Dalai Lama looks are a little less important, but we have not achieved such nobility of mind on this side of the ocean.

Yes! Both Jdate and Match.com sent a notice that my photos had been accepted and would appear on the sites.[41]

---

40 My mind conjures images of hunched, wizard-like gnomes dressed in long gowns like Dumbledore, moving chess pieces around a board with the wave of a wand, smiling all the time with sadistic glee.

41 It's humbling to know that you are at the mercy of some twenty-something office worker, legs up on the desk, flicking through photos that in your mind represent the best you have to offer, while he/she is yawning and scrolling through your glamour shots with one hand and rifling through a bag of Chicken McNuggets with the other.

Now it was a waiting game. Not a long one, though. My dedication in drafting an appealing profile and choosing my photos paid off almost immediately, and "hearts," "flirts," "likes," quips, and comments rolled in on both sites. Lord have mercy, what a load of crap speeds through cyberspace on these websites. The purveyors of said crap were all there in force: the zanies, the flakes, the weirdoes, the nerds, the grownup boys still looking for momma, the pompous asses, the creatures from the Black Lagoon and all of their kin who troll for prey on dating sites. One such message expressed a fervent hope that I would be willing to chase squirrels naked in the woods with him, a hope that, sadly, remains unfulfilled.

If this sounds one sided, pointing the finger at men while implying that women on dating sites are the model of stability and maturity, that's not intentional. What's good for the goose is good for the gander, and while the issues may be different, it is my firm belief that as many women out there are unstable and immature as men. The thing is, men are the only ones on my radar, so I've got no data in the other direction.

Among the eccentric messages I received were several that were more mainstream, but initially even those were disappointing, authored by men who wanted actual dates. Conversation. Dinner. Can you imagine? Where's that guy who just wants casual sex when you need him?

After a week without the hoped-for response, worry set in. The law of diminishing returns is a big concern in Internet dating. Fresh meat gets a lot of attention, but after two or three weeks the attention drops, dwindling to almost nothing after a couple of months unless a woman does something drastic to make herself "new" again—for example, a photo with her skirt blowing up around her head like Marilyn Monroe, preferably without panties. Resolving to be patient, I went about my business, checking for new hits every few hours. Ten days out, curled up on the sofa at home, my patience was rewarded. Benjamin's email was funny and clever with a slightly sexual overtone: "I like your profile, want to make a dishonest man out of me?"

That made me grin. A sex object with a good sense of humor? Now we're talking. Time for a celebration. Out came one of my favorite wine glasses, a clear glass goblet with a colored stem that I'd bought at a craft show, and in went a healthy serving of cold, crisp Chardonnay. That hit the spot. Back to the sofa, I opened my laptop and clicked on Benjamin's name.

Here's a piece of advice: don't ever swallow wine when you think you might get a surprise, because if you start choking, the acid in the wine will close up your throat. After much gasping and choking, the tears cleared from my eyes and I started laughing. Benjamin lived in Israel. That shouldn't have been such a surprise, because the same thing had happened more than once on JDate. Understandably, it was easily forgotten, because then as now it seemed so ridiculous. What did these Israeli men really want? A Jewish woman, that much was clear. Okay, fine. Were there no Jewish women in Israel? Only a few million. Did these men expect irresistible American Jewesses to hop on a plane to Israel for a date? A domestic flight, okay,[42] but international travel for a blind date? Call me unreasonable, but no.

Back to the drawing board. No other gems came in that night or the next couple of days. Never mind, it was spring, and I was in a great mood. This was a good time to get myself in shape for my elusive lover. Bored with the usual indoor exercise options and given the great weather, buying a bike seemed like a good idea. Nothing fancy or complicated, a solid but girly Beach Cruiser would do nicely, which I found without difficulty at a nearby bike shop. Add a pink and white striped helmet and a bell to the hot pink bike I had selected and it was workout time. Riding around the parking lot and down the street, headphones on and rocking out to my favorite music didn't seem like exercise at all. Most any activity with music is a good time. Live is the best, but recorded will do: Allman Brothers, Springsteen, Beyoncé, the Doors, Guns N' Roses, Hendrix, Led Zeppelin, Marvin Gaye. . . . The list goes on and on, because music takes me out of my head and calms my often-chattering mind like few other things can. Hot yoga and alcohol come to mind, but the first is sweaty and disgusting and if you want to see the definition of a sloppy drunk, watch me overindulge in the second.

---

42 Guilty with an explanation. When I was fixed up during my time in a graduate program in Miami, I flew to Jacksonville for the night, because (a) in those days I was entitled beyond measure and (b) it was a cool adventure, even if it turned out to be a lousy date.

After a few days, my butt was feeling a little tighter, but still no luck on the dating sites. Then, like magic, up popped an email from Mark the Musician. How serendipitous was that? Me biking around and all into my music, and the universe just spits out a musician. A guitar player no less. Be still my beating heart. He hadn't posted a photo, but so what? He was a musician!

Mark and I agreed to meet for a drink at a reasonably trendy bar the very next night. Hot to trot! That was a good sign. Choosing what to wear was problematic. Dressing for any blind date was a challenge, but now I had the added pressure of wanting to look a little slutty. Slutty was not really my strong suit. Lawyer attire, funky concert garb, evening out dress up, all of that came naturally. Slutty? That was outside my comfort zone. Normally a call to Nancy or one of my other girlfriends would have solved the problem, but not wanting to explain myself nixed that. *Us Weekly* was coming to me regularly for reasons unknown, and what worked quite well in their pages for younger women provided a pretty good template for slutty at my age, too. Anything incredibly tight that outlined my crotch would do. That was easy, since my closet was full of clothes two sizes too small. A woman has to be prepared for fluctuations in weight, and theoretically what goes up can come down. So, it's important to hang on to the smaller sizes, not just the larger ones. Big deal if they haven't been worn in, say, five years? You never know when a life-threatening illness will rid you of fifteen or twenty pounds.

It was early June, but the nights were still a little cool, so jeans and a sweater sounded about right. Not just any old jeans and sweater mind you, super skinny, super tight jeans and a dramatically low-cut top. With the bar just around the corner, I timed my arrival to make a suitably dramatic late entrance. Asking for Mark at the hostess station, she directed me to a high-top outside. Did the hostess narrow her eyes as she spoke or was that just a trick of the light? Huh. Whatever. The real issue was whether to sit inside or out. The evening was warm, so even in my generally sweatless state, sweat was a possibility. On the other hand, the breeze would lift my hair, always an attractive look. Oops, trying for slutty, not attractive. Dip my hair over one eye? But then I was blind in that eye. That wasn't comfortable. Screw it, the tight jeans and the boob action would have to do the trick.

Turning the corner to the outside deck, I looked around. There was a vagrant sitting at one table, a well-dressed man at another and couples at every other table. Why did they let a vagrant enter such an upscale, trendy bar, I wondered? The mirrored counters and posters of colorful modern art spoke of style and taste. The owner must be a charitable person. That was nice.

Approaching the well-dressed man, I stuck out my hand and said, "Hi, you must be Mark."

"You must have the wrong person. My name isn't Mark."

My date couldn't be the vagrant. Where was the other single man I must have missed in scanning the tables?

Nobody. Hoping against hope that my date was in the bathroom, I went over to the vagrant's table. Keeping my hand to myself, I inquired, "Are you by any chance Mark?" Neil Young looked good compared to this guy,[43] so when he said "Yes," it was all I could do not to bolt. As usual, good manners won. I introduced myself and sat down, wondering how soon this could end.

How fast was the fastest date you've ever had? Speed dating doesn't count. Mark was eight minutes. Mark didn't like me any better than I liked him. My failings are unknown to me. How about clean hair? Perfume? We didn't even order a drink, since calling it an early night was a no brainer. At seven minutes fifty-nine seconds, murmuring, "Nice to meet you, but I don't think this is a fit," I backed away from the table, preparing to field Mark's response. No need. His face remained blank as a slate and, unlike me, apparently no compulsion to be courteous afflicted him. Was he in a stupor? The answer remained a mystery, as I continued to back-pedal until I was out of sight and on the way to my car. Hazel looked puzzled when I came home only twenty-two minutes into the *Game of Thrones* episode I'd left on for her, but darling that she is, she turned her attention from Jon

---

43   Sorry, Neil, I'm a huge fan, none bigger, but you've got to admit you've got an intensely scruffy thing going on. Darryl Hannah doesn't seem to mind and more power to her, but some things are just fact. Who cares anyway when you've been making the best music around for decades?

Neil, if you are reading this, could you please do more concerts with Crazy Horse? And I do hope the "scruffy" comment didn't offend you. I really am an admirer.

Snow—a visual feast for any female—and jumped down to greet me.

Reflecting on the evening, perhaps it was time to give up. Twice in a row I had gotten excited then had the wind taken out of my sails. Still, they say that the third time is the charm. Maybe my luck would turn.

Sure enough, five days later, another fish took the bait. His name was Peter. Though cautious about getting my hopes up, at least I liked the name. Peter. The name rolled around on my tongue. Oh yes, I could screw someone named Peter. George would have been a different story. The Georges in my life so far had been heroes, noble gentlemen all, and I would not sully their name with my descent into the sex trade, so to speak. No Waynes either; as the name of my children's father, that would have been disrespectful. Peter, on the other hand, held no such connections and had a nice ring, not to mention the obvious play on words.[44] Right out of the gate Peter was chatting sexual innuendo. "Hey, good lookin', I'm really into you.

---

44   In our culture, many common men's names are slang for the male member. There is a scholarly discussion of this phenomenon in footnote 32, which I know you read and remember well.

I'm sorry, you don't remember that footnote? Perhaps you skipped it in your haste to finish the chapter? Oh, I see, not just that one, you skipped them all? Go back and read them. There will be a quiz. Think of them like the icing on the cake, the cherry on top of the sundae. What would dessert be without them?

If, on the other hand, you actually were in need of an explanation concerning the connection between the name Peter and a penis, that's a more significant problem. The solution escapes me. Stash a secret microphone in a men's locker room? Watch *Austin Powers: The Spy Who Shagged Me* several times? Ask any ten-year-old boy?

I especially liked what you said about being open sexually. Hit me back."

Good, very promising. Let's see his profile. Location? Check. Peter lived right here in Atlanta. Photo? Check. You couldn't really see much because his face was at an angle and shadowed, but he looked tall and reasonably well built. Certainly nothing like the vagrant. Now for the rest of his profile. Oh. Oh my. He's how young? Could it be? Holy cow. Young. Very young. As in twenty-eight years younger than me young. I could have been his mother. This kid was only seven years older than my son, for heaven's sake.

Moment of truth. Was I ready to be a cougar?

What did that even mean, really? Ever a vocabulary buff, I investigated.

Definition #1: "An older woman who frequents clubs in order to score with a much younger man. The cougar can be anyone from a surgically altered wind tunnel victim, to an absolute sad and bloated old horn-meister, to a real hottie or milf.[45] Cougars are gaining in popularity—particularly the true hotties—as young men find not only a sexual high, but many times a chick with her shit together."[46]

Wow. What did that all mean? Horn-meister? Milf? It all sounded a little frightening. Not like me at all.

---

45 "MILF" stands for "Mother I'd Like to Fuck." https://en.wikipedia.org/wiki/MILF_(slang)

Just thought you'd like to know.

46 http://www.urbandictionary.com/define.php?term=Cougar

Not to be deterred, further research produced:

Definition #2: "Cougar is a slang term referring to a woman who seeks sexual activity with younger men."[47]

That sounded better. Pretty neutral, no talk about "surgically altered wind tunnel victims" and such. More like a business transaction, and those were right up my alley. My family operated a business and I'd grown up hearing the ins and outs discussed every night at the dinner table. Yeah, okay, this was just like selling brassieres.[48] That, I could do.

Once past the cougar hurdle, other revelations of interest appeared in Peter's profile. Scanning his profile, my eyes lighted on the news that he was from a Dutch background, in fact born in Holland, then moved to the United States as a twenty-year-old. Splendid! This brought back fond memories of Rikke, a sophisticated young man my aunt and uncle had invited for a home exchange when I was a teenager. Talk about good looking. Rikke had been totally hot, in a Matthew McConaughey kind of way, and unconsciously stylish in that insouciant manner that European men seem to be gifted with from birth. Not to mention such a sexy accent! It was summertime of my fifteenth year, and Rikke's body in a European speedo-style bathing suit sparked new sensations *down there*. My

---

47   https://en.wikipedia.org/wiki/Cougar_(slang)

48   I didn't use the word "brassieres" by accident. That actually was the family business, from the 1920s till the 1990s. If you don't believe me look up "The Lovable Company." In grammar school, I gave petit pants—there's a blast from the past—as gifts to my girlfriends.

yearnings for Rikke went unrequited, but the daydreams they spawned were all the more satisfying to my puerile mind. If Peter was anything like Rikke, this was going to be a literal and figurative ball.[49] To top it off, one of Peter's interests was watching football. That was a sign of masculinity to me, and a nice association with my father, who loved football and took me to every college or pro game in the City of Atlanta between 1961 and 1971 when I went away to college.[50]

Let the games begin.

---

49   Probably showing my age again, "Wanna ball?" was one of a number of eloquent propositions favored by the boys when I was in my late teens, the common denominator being that almost all of them began with "Wanna."

50   This seems like an appropriate time to memorialize a completely irrelevant but vastly amusing cheer from my father's high school that may well have inspired his ongoing love of the game:

"Alla bin. Alla bin. Alla bin diego, san diego, rachas sachas kiss my tuchas,* Boys High! Boys High! Rah! Rah! Rah!"

*Pronounced "tachas," "tuchas" means "ass." You guessed it, more Yiddish. If the cheer sounds dated, it is, but in 1936 it was cool as can be for the Jewish kids who chanted it.

I will pay fifty dollars to anyone who heard that cheer in the flesh and can prove it. Don't lie.

CHAPTER TWO

———— ❧ ————

Hear Me Roar

Communicating by written message is so easy, isn't it? Simply open the dating app, read the message, sit back and dream up a great response. The right words might escape me on the spot, but via message there was ample time to think them up. Assistance from my friend and frequent companion, the Online Thesaurus, was just a click away. No pressure, no live person to deal with, just words on a screen. Piece of cake.

Initiating contact with Peter was easy, because this part of the dating ritual was habit in the online dating universe. The only wild card was his age. How to communicate with a guy that young?

The trick was a message that had a younger flavor but still felt like me. Okay, that was familiar from my kids' texts in the family group chat.

"Hey, what's up? I'm just getting dressed to go out. It was nice to hear from you."

There was no reply message right away, so I headed out to the movies with a friend. Rule follower that I am, normally my phone would be on silent, not even vibrate, the moment I entered the theater, but this was a special occasion. A message from Peter might arrive any second and being available for that trumped good manners by a mile.

Once we were seated I put my phone on vibrate and settled in to divide my time between watching the movie and checking for messages. It was an irritating way to watch a movie, but my diligence was rewarded when thirty minutes into the film a little "1" appeared atop the app. "Okay good." I thought. "He swallowed the hook. Now all I have to do is reel him in."

Opening the app, I clicked on the message: "Hey. Glad you hit me back. You are so hot. I really got off on thinking about you getting dressed. Let's go off line. Text me at ###-###-####."

Uh oh, maybe I was a little hasty congratulating myself on reeling the fish in, because this particular fisherman had absolutely no idea how to respond to the fish. First thought: "Thank you, that was so nice of you to say!" After all, I was taught to always say thank you to a compliment. Scratch that, time to put Miss Manners in the closet and channel the Kardashians.

"Same," I texted to the number he'd sent. Sometimes less is more, so I let that one fly without any embellishment.

Peter responded, "Cool, great minds think alike, right? Do you have any pics?"

"Nope, you?"

"What do you want to see?"

How did I respond? I can't remember but recall quite clearly my feeling of panic and that by this time I had moved to the lobby out of guilt over having my phone screen lit for so long. I remember watching the popcorn machine behind the concessions counter slowly fill with popped corn as I texted something about waiting to see each other in the flesh, and off we went into banter that quickly morphed into sexting. Keeping up my end was a struggle, but I managed to answer Peter's texts by crafting carefully thought out responses that appeared oh so spontaneous. That works just fine when the person on the other end can neither see you nor hear you. Anyway, Peter didn't care as long as the ball was moving toward the end zone.

This went on for a couple of days, with him sending texts almost constantly. How people hold down a job while doing this is beyond me. For my part, I ignored Peter's messages during the daytime and filled those hours drafting language for complicated contracts. My nights were spent catching up with his messages and composing sexy return salvos. It was exhausting. Most of what we said is lost to the mists of time, but for one nugget, memorable for its shock value.

On the third night, Peter texted me, "Do you squirt?"

What? What could that mean? I had no idea. Summoning my finely-honed research skills, I typed "sex woman squirt" into the browser on my laptop.

The response that popped up on my screen almost gave me a coronary:

"Squirt: *female ejaculation* ... kind of. It refers to the moment when a woman has an orgasm, and liquid literally squirts out from down there. 'Squirters' are exactly what they sound like: *girls who can squirt during orgasm*. However, squirting is also pretty controversial because, um... the jury is out on whether it's real or not." [51]

Yuck! Yuck, yuck, yuck! The description conjured visions of milk squirting from a cow's udder. Was this true? Did women really squirt? My friends didn't do this, or if they did, they never told me, and believe me, we talk about *everything*. Not in books, not in movies, not on TV, not anywhere had I ever heard of this phenomenon. A quick phone call to Nancy to spot check: yep, it was news to her, too.

Back to Peter: "No, I don't. I'm fifty-eight years old, and that's not really part of the game at this point. Are you sure you're cool with my age?" He didn't need to know that (a) this had never been part of my game, (b) I didn't really believe it, and (c) if it was true, it sounded really gross. Was I that out of touch? Considering that I am a middle-aged

---

51 How can you doubt a source as reliable as "gurl.com?' I know I can't. http://www.gurl.com/2014/08/23/what-is-squirting-female-orgasm-advice/#ixzz4MdxK5box

mother of three, lawyer and quasi-princess, naiveté was a definite possibility. Cover my dismay and stay in the game, I thought. The stakes, after all, were high.

Peter assured me he was fine with my age, and in fact, he couldn't wait to get in my pants. Thank heavens, my status as a non-squirter was not a deal breaker. Imagine my relief.

Still, a host of competing thoughts bombarded me: Did I really want to pull the trigger on a sexual encounter with a stranger? What about safety? Was I truly excited to sleep with Peter or just pretending? What were the pros and what were the cons? Typical lawyer, I made a decision tree, and the pros (my libido) won the day. "Yes! Hell yes! It's time for sex and it's time for adventure. I'm bored and horny and if I don't do something, it's never going to change."

Done. I texted Peter to come over the following Tuesday. This was Friday and I was going out of town for the weekend. Monday was a day to catch up on work, so Tuesday was my first window of opportunity.

Tuesday worked for Peter, too. Though perhaps Tuesday would have worked for Peter unless he was having lung transplant surgery in the morning, in which case I'm pretty sure he would have been available in the afternoon. We agreed to meet at 10:30 a.m. in the parking lot outside the security gate of my complex. Not particularly cautious by nature—ya think?—this seemed like the intelligent thing to do.

Off on my weekend trip, daydreams of hard pecs and harder erections floated through my mind. The airplane seat was vibrating in time with me, I felt so excited, so hot and turned on. Tuesday couldn't come soon enough for me.

CHAPTER THREE

Miaow

What about my pets? When should I go down to the parking lot? And the usual, what to wear? So many questions. The pets were easy. My cat, Ace, was an indoor-outdoor cat and wouldn't mind staying out for a few hours since the weather was fine. Hazel was a big fan of doggy daycare, so I dropped her at a location around the corner from my house.

What to wear was more of a test. A bra-let and shorts? A thong and stilettos? This was worse than getting ready for the date with Mark the Musician. If life to this point had not prepared me for dressing like a slut, it double damn sure hadn't prepared me for dressing for a sexual encounter with a stranger twenty-eight years my junior.

Pulling one outfit after another out of the closet, nothing seemed right. My anxiety level climbed even though this was supposed to be fun, something for my own entertainment and gratification. Why so much stress?

Was there a teensy bit of inner conflict about this little adventure? Maybe suppressing a little fear that my less-than-taut fifty-eight-year-old skin was going to turn off a young stud? Maybe this wasn't going to work out the way I intended? Worst of all, was the encounter putting me in a vulnerable position where I might get hurt?

Sure, all those things were true. But this train had left the station and it was not turning back. No way. Wild sex was on the horizon and I deserved to have it. Not tomorrow or next week, but today. Screw the clothes. They would all be on the floor soon enough anyway. As for nerves, there was only one thing to do. Pulling out the Valium I had stashed a few years ago, I poured a glass of water and took one. Hmm. One probably wasn't enough. Seeing how anxious I felt, better pop another.

At this stage of my life, psych meds no longer held a place in my recovery toolkit. There was a time when there wasn't an anti-depressant or anti-anxiety med I wouldn't try, and courtesy of various prescribers, occasionally in cocktails of three or four interacting drugs at one time.[52] When I finally figured out that for me there was no magic

---

52   Psych meds for depression and/or anxiety played a big part in my life from 1982 until 2010. Then I wrote *Southern Vapors* and became a multi-millionaire best-selling author and mental health advocate and stopped taking psych meds. Just kidding, still waiting on the multi-millionaire best-selling author part, but the rest is true.

bullet, I stopped taking those meds, but held on to a few bottles with recent prescriptions. Including Valium.[53] Sure, I hadn't taken anything like that for a while, but the results in the past had been quick and my reactions predictable. Nervous jitters? Poof, up in smoke. Inhibitions? Gone, and I do mean gone. After a few minutes, who would care what Peter thought about the old body? Together we would climb to the heights of ecstasy and no doubt he would forget what week it was, much less notice a wrinkle here or a pucker there. Time to rock and roll.

There was just one teensy little problem with the path I had just chosen. While my release from inhibitions and anxiety was guaranteed, my tolerance level for Valium after not taking it for so long was unknown, and who knew the stability of the drug after a few years in my kitchen drawer? Sure, my reactions were predictable when the drug was carefully introduced into my system and my body chemistry given a chance to acclimate. But there had been that time a long while ago, something about a bad reaction to Valium, what was that again? Oh yeah. That.

As a young lawyer, one day at work I began to feel awful, as if there was a stone sitting on my chest making it impossible to draw a deep breath. A quick call to my family physician produced a prescription for Valium, although in its generic name so the type of drug didn't register with me when I filled the prescription at a nearby pharmacy.

---

53 I always had a soft spot for Valium after I heard The Rolling Stones' *Mother's Little Helper*. It had such a ring of truth, even to my uncommonly naïve teenage ears.

Presumably he had diagnosed a good old-fashioned panic attack and figured that a dose of Valium would set me right. The fact that I'd never before taken the drug or any drug of its class seemingly was no impediment in my physician's view.

He certainly missed the boat on that one. Fifteen or twenty minutes after I took the prescribed dose, I walked down the hall to deliver a document to a partner's office. It quickly became apparent that the simple act of perambulation was beyond me, as I lurched down the corridor bouncing off desks to the opposing wall and back like a pinball. It felt like floating in and out of an altered reality in which the edges of things were softer and it was hard to stay focused. Only later did I put two and two together and ascribe my symptoms to the Valium. At the time, I only knew that I had to leave the office and go home to bed.

In all of the intervening years and periods of experimentation with psych meds, I'd forgotten that little episode. Until now, when without warning it became a matter of some urgency to remember it. Because to my dismay, that same sense of altered reality was intruding with the same alacrity. A split second later, it was too late. I—specifically my prefrontal cortex—was already MIA.[54]

Alrighty then. The choice of clothes had gotten a whole lot easier, but getting into them was suddenly quantum physics. It took a while, stumbling around the apartment,

---

54 How often do two blatant footnote opportunities present themselves in the space of five words (six if you count the dash)? You can thank me later for giving you the benefit of the doubt on both.

hopping on one leg, until the whole point came back to me—to put both legs in my pants and then walk. Every once in a while, my watch reminded me of the rendez-vous time with Peter. Time passed fast then slowly, in a stretchy, elastic way. Speaking of elastic, the hands on my watch stretched over the edge of the casing and spilled out on to my wrists. How interesting. Man, Salvador Dali knew what he was doing when he painted that melting clock.[55]

At some point, Peter was supposed to text me when he was almost to the parking lot where we were to meet. A wave of panic sloshed over me. Had I missed the time? No, it was only 10:00 a.m. and we were sup-posed to meet at 10:30 a.m. Still, Peter should have tex-ted me by now. As part of my brain registered a feeling of upset, almost immediately a blue and white vase on a low table in the corner of my den became a distraction. Look at that, the wavy pattern was so cool. Funny how the Valium worked—all of my jitters gone, perfectly content to stare at a vase. Why again did I give that up?

"Look at your phone. Has he texted?"

The functional part of my brain desperately tried to be responsible. No, Peter hadn't texted. What time was

---

55 "Persistence of Memory," painted by Salvador Dali in 1931 in the midst of a hallucination, is one of the world's best-known paintings and an icon of contemporary art. My generation always thinks we invented every-thing, like psychedelic trips and free love and revolutionary music and anything else you can think of. Ha. There really is nothing new under the sun. Except maybe the Internet. And gel nail polish, which is the coolest thing because it never chips.

it? Good grief, it was 10:20 a.m. Get in the car and drive down to the parking lot.

At that moment, the phone rang. Saved by the bell! But the screen revealed it was only a call from my doctor's office. I was waiting to hear the results on a big deal eye exam, but there was no way to answer that call. Why did reality (in its unaltered form) always seem to intrude at the worst time? How should I handle this? Ignore the call? Yeah, ignore it. Good, right, yeah. After a few more seconds the phone stopped ringing. Good, time to relax.

No. No relaxing. What if the doctor's office was leaving a voice mail at this very moment? What if it was something really important? Should I call them back? Could I even speak coherently? Probably not. No, definitely not.

Time passed, maybe seconds, maybe minutes. Still no message. After a minute or two, I relaxed and the state of wellbeing returned, along with thoughts of killer sex with Peter. Where was his text? Where was he?

Oh, there was that idea before the call from the doctor's office. What was it? Something to do with a car. That's it, drive to the parking lot! It was just down the hill and one right turn into the parking lot. Anybody could do that.

So, I did. I am not proud of the fact that I drove while under the influence, but I did. At least it was only down the hill to the parking lot. The trip seemed to go well, but for a constant refrain that sounded vaguely like cymbals clashed at random intervals. Always a fan of the percussion section, my only thought was "How nice, and I didn't even have to turn on the radio." Later, when I had to buy a new wheel because my right front tire had hit the curb countless times, it wasn't so amusing, but such mundane considerations were irrelevant at the time.

Arriving with the car mostly intact, I parked near the front of the lot, better to see Peter when he arrived. Sitting there, in a flash of lucidity, it came to me that until this moment I had given no thought to Peter himself, beyond associating him with the Rikke, the fascinating Dutch boy from my youth. How odd, to be waiting for a stranger who would soon be in my bed.

Huh?

The curtain of fog closed back up and I sat in a near stupor for the next few minutes. Rousing myself, my watch now read 10:35 a.m. Where was Peter? Maybe I should text him. Okay, good move.

"Hey, Peter, where are you? Are you on your way?"

"I'm here. Where are you?"

"You're here? Here where?"

"I'm in the parking lot, just like you said."

What? Peter—in the parking lot? I was in the parking lot. Peter wasn't.

Was he?

Two rows behind me in the corner next to some empty tennis courts sat a dented black pick-up truck. Not the kind of pick-up truck that is so popular these days, with giant tires that sit way up off the ground and names like "F-150 Platinum." An old model that had seen better days, but was never a looker even in its infancy. Time to use the voice function of my phone. Despite being stoned out of my gourd, I managed to dial Peter's number, expecting an urbane Dutch accent to greet me when he answered.

"Huhllo?"

Even stoned, something in that one word seemed amiss. "Peter, is that you?"

"Yup. Ahm just sittin' over heeyar in mah truhck."

Hold on. This guy sounded like the biggest cracker ever. Through the haze, it dawned that I had never actually heard Peter's voice. Our entire flirtation had been carried on via text. Oh, my God. What an idiot I was. It hadn't occurred to me that the way Peter looked or talked would matter. After all, what difference did that make? All I wanted was sex, right?

But it did make a difference. I'd imagined Peter as a reincarnation of Rikke, down to the way he spoke English. Somehow, an attachment and a whole set of false expectations created that totally artificial construct. Almost immediately, the feeling of calm started to evaporate, replaced by swirling dread.

Peter was still on the phone. "Yuh want ta go own and drahve up the hiyull to yer place?"

Help me, Jesus, what butchery of the English language. What part of Holland was this guy from again? Such a reaction to the way Peter talked may seem snobby and downright bitchy, but remember my struggle with the knight in shining armor syndrome? That casual tendency to embrace fantasy over reality when relating to men? Yes, that. Without realizing it, the fantasy had won yet again. Not only was Peter supposed to be like Rikke, he was supposed to throw me over the saddle of his horse and, metaphorically, take me to his castle. He wasn't supposed to be real and have flaws, for heaven's sake.

Judging his accent as a flaw was the product of my early education at the hands of my northern mother, who intensely disliked "Southern English." The first time she heard me say "Ah" in pronouncing the word "I" as a child, she devoted herself to eradicating any flat vowels from my speech. After long hours repeating "Eye," it became second nature, along with a measure of her own negative opinion.[56]

Frantically pushing through the fog, my brain lagged behind, still on autopilot. On the verge of saying yes and going up the hill to my apartment with Peter, a sager part of me bought a little time by asking, "I tell you what, why don't we get out of our cars and meet each other?"

"How come?"

"I just think it's a good idea."

"Uh, okay."

With monumental trepidation, I watched in fascination as the door to the pick-up truck swung open. One blue jeaned leg appeared, then two. Peter's whole body came into view as he climbed out of the truck. Literally climbed. The truck, even such an old model, was too tall for Peter, or he was too short for the truck, depending on your point of view. What happened to the tall guy in the photo on the dating website? Frozen in place, I looked hard at him. Forget short or tall, he was a boy. A kid. He

---

56 In a rare display of rebellion, I refused to give up "y"all, or "all a y'all." One has to draw the line somewhere.

still had pimples. He had on jeans and a t-shirt, not even a cool t-shirt like the Dive Bar t-shirts I like to buy for my son.[57] An off-white (dirty?) t-shirt, no design, just plain. Accompanied by a baseball cap turned backwards and a pair of flip-flops, which served well to highlight the dirt under his toenails.

That did it. No way. A redneck kid barely dry behind the ears? Uh-uh. Besides, what was this little weasel doing trolling the internet for women like me?[58] Had he actually succeeded in previous seductions? I shuddered to think of the possibilities. No amount of Valium could induce me to add to Peter's success rate, but I wasn't happy about delivering the message. After all, I had invited him over to have sex. He might get angry when I reneged, and I was in no shape to deal with that.

"Hey, you reyuddy?" Peter said. He'd halted uncertainly, perhaps in reaction to my body language. By this time I was in full flight mode.

"Peter," I said, "I'm sorry but this isn't happening."

"Huh?"

"This isn't happening," I repeated, somehow restraining the impulse to add, "But thanks for coming."

---

57   Check it out: https://www.divebarshirtclub.com/NewWeb/Web/
Default.asp?SessID={CB0355FB-0FFF-46EF-A04C-45D2851DA43E}
&RandID=3296 "T-shirts from the best bars you've never heard of." Way cool, right?

58   Hmm. Perhaps a better question was what was *I* doing on the Internet trolling for boys like Peter. Caught in the throes of Valium-fueled disappointment, the thought didn't occur to me until later.

"Oh. Uh. Okay." Peter turned around and shuffled back to his truck.

Was it going to be that easy? Yes, thankfully it was. Peter simply got back in his truck—with a little hoist from the leather strap hanging above the door—reversed out of his parking space and drove away.

Back in my car, I leaned against the steering wheel and cranked the engine. Shock may not be the right word to describe my state, but it sure felt like a ringing blow to the head. To top it off, maybe as a result of an adrenaline rush induced by my encounter with Peter, the Valium was beginning to wear off, leaving me a little less foggy but a lot more unnerved.

Back up the hill inside my apartment, it was a comfort to be safe and sound in my own surroundings. Trying to come back to myself, a very long, very hot shower helped, but work was out of the question. Thankfully I was in a rare slow spot and had no pressing projects, so a day off was not a problem. The afternoon stretched before me and, still a little shaken, I burrowed into my ever-welcoming sofa and dozed off for a couple of hours. When I awoke, I was relieved to discover that I felt clear headed and refreshed, so I got dressed and headed to a nearby grocery store. Surely I was competent to handle the choice between chicken thighs and ground turkey. The drive to Publix was a piece of cake, which reinforced my conclusion that everything was back to normal. Wrong again. Without warning, right as I walked up to the meat counter, some residual chemical in my body kicked back in, which became evident when I lurched to the side, held erect only by my death grip on the handle of the grocery cart. All I could do was stand and stare at the packages of chicken. To top it off, my rapt attention to the chicken display must have caught the butcher's eye, because at some point it penetrated my addled brain that a man wearing a white apron had asked more than once if he could help me. Pulling myself together with an effort, I mumbled, "Thanks, not right now." Giving me a puzzled look, he nodded and replied, "Please let me know if you change your mind."

What mind? My mind had checked out and left the Valium in charge. The best I could do was grab my purse out of the cart and flee to the Starbucks located next to the grocery store. Forty-five minutes and two Mochaccinos later, I was wired to the gills—that's a near lethal quantity of espresso for someone who gave up caffeine in 1986—but unquestionably returned to reality and able to safely drive the short distance home. Hazel stayed close, perhaps sensing, as dogs do, that some TLC was needed. For another two hours I paced the house, fueled by all the caffeine I had consumed, but finally I wore myself out, climbed into bed and drifted off to sleep, my last conscious thought: "Some of us are cut out to be house cats, not cougars."

INTERLUDE

Random Online Dating Message

MAN: *You should get a massage and be ready for anything this New Years. Don't let lack of affection and loneliness make you thornier than a dozen red roses. I'm tall kind, and affectionate and warm so don't become sexually frustrated. I'm not the biggest guy . . . but I'm proud of every foot. If you have a few extra pounds I can be your personal trainer, you can roll out of bed and right into your morning workout and you're already warmed up! You will always be first. Put away the toys and lock "Bill Doe" back in the closet and wrap yourself around a good, strong well dressed man with tempurpedic lips, big heart and a big jackson.*

Random Online Dating Message

MAN: *You seem like an open-minded lady. Would you be willing to check out a website to see if we have things in common?*

WOMAN: *Sure, just send me the link and I'll look it up.*

MAN: *Here ya go. www.xyz.com* [not really]

MAN: *Did you look it up? What did you think? What are you into?*

WOMAN: *Well, for starters one thing I'm into is wearing clothes, so I don't think this is going to work.* [The website depicted a nudist colony for middle-aged people.]

Random Online Dating Message

WOMAN: *Ms. Maxwell . . . my name is Mrs. Michael Grambling . . . yep he is married. I am also copying him so that he knows I sent you this. He does not live in Atlanta as his profile states nor is he divorced. At least not yet. This is the about the 4th site he has registered for in the last 2 years and every time i get the "im sorry, never again . ." speech. You want him? You can have him.*

PART FOUR

George

CHAPTER ONE

A Nice Introduction

My law practice occasionally took me to out-of-the-way spots, including a visit in late October to West Texas to consult for a small regional hospital. The work was memorable only for the level of recalcitrance exhibited by the client, but the flight home was a pleasure. Switching airlines from Southwest to Delta to make an earlier flight was a good decision. What a treat not boarding the plane by cattle call: an assigned chair to call my own![59]

---

59 Not to be disloyal to Southwest, I fly them all the time. No change fees! Heaven. Not having a seat assignment does get old, though, and I'm too stubborn to add to my cheap fare by paying for a boarding spot.

Being seated next to an intriguing looking female hipster who appeared to be around my age was another improvement. Halloween was around the corner, so I broke the ice by asking if she was ready for trick or treaters.

"Nope, not interested in ankle-biters, didn't even know it was Halloween," she replied. "Now that you've reminded me, I'll be on the lookout for the Halloween Oreos—the orange filling is the bomb. Hi, by the way, I'm Julie." Oh ho, she was just my cup of tea, except for the child hater part. Her nonchalant air was matched by her black mink hat and golden velvet pants that looked like a retro nod to Carnaby Street[60] in the 1960s. Julie's dangling silver earrings looked like miniature versions of the studded maces that warriors swung at their enemies in the Middle Ages. As a sucker for outré style, a major girl crush overcame me.

We chatted off and on during the flight and after landing were still engaged in conversation as the plane rolled up to the gate. To my surprise, the flight attendant came over and said that a wheelchair would be at the plane's exit in just a minute if Julie didn't mind waiting. When I asked what was wrong, she told me without inflection that she'd been diagnosed with multiple sclerosis in her twenties and had been largely wheelchair bound for years. My girl crush morphed into true admiration

---

60 The birthplace of hip, Carnaby Street was described by Time Magazine in 1966 as the epicenter of "the new swinging London, crammed with a cluster of the 'gear' boutiques where the girls and boys buy each other clothing." *Time Magazine*, April 15, 1966.

for a person who didn't wear her affliction on her sleeve and moved through life with style and aplomb in the face of it. Talk about a role model.

Once Julie was settled in the wheelchair, I walked beside her to baggage claim. With a few things in common, including recently acquired puppies, we had plenty to talk about and pictures to share of my hound dog mix, Augie,[61] and her Pug, Harley.

Sad to say, Hazel, sidekick and comfort of my leanest years, went to her final rest soon after my failed tryst with Peter. It seemed she was never the same after her encounter with Cyrus. Some things are too much to be borne by man or beast. Sending her to her final rest was painful in the extreme, but like any true dog lover, another rescue pet stole my heart a few months later. Augie entered my life, a goofy, silly, loving, mostly hound dog puppy.

As we waited for our luggage, Julie asked, "Would you like to come to a party at my house this weekend? It's for my birthday dinner group, some work friends and family. The group takes turns celebrating birthdays at different

---

61 Remember Augie Doggie and Doggie Daddy on "The Quick Draw McGraw Show?" When I rescued a dog that was predominantly American Foxhound, I had to name him Augie.

Now those were the days of great cartoons: "The Huckleberry Hound Show," "Yogi Bear," "Jonny Quest," "The Flintstones," "The Jetsons," "The Bugs Bunny Show" and generally any Merrie Melodies cartoon were my favorites. Not that all of the later 'toons were bad—"SpongeBob SquarePants" is a classic and no one should miss "Courage the Cowardly Dog," a little known, side-splittingly funny and clever cartoon that ran from 1996 to 2002. Wikipedia describes the latter as an "animated horror comedy television series," which probably tells you something about me.

houses, and this month I'm hosting my own birthday with the guests of my choice at home."

"Sure," I said, "That sounds great." Julie gave me her address and the date and time of the party and we parted company.

On the appointed night, Siri Victoria's[62] directions took me a fair distance to a newly built community outside the "Perimeter," as the ring road that surrounds Atlanta is known. After half an hour, I arrived at her house, a Cape Cod beauty nestled behind two still fragrant box-wood gardens replete with late-flowering roses at the tail end of their season. The front door was painted a vibrant Chinese red and sported a lacquered black knocker in the shape of a large teardrop that seemed just the edgy deco-rating touch to be expected of Julie. A man answered after one bang of the heavy knocker. He looked to be about my age and bore a passing resemblance to Julie.

"Hi," he said, "I'm George, Julie's brother." Bingo. "Can I get you a drink?"

George was silver haired, of medium height, and chunky. He was not particularly good looking, except for his eyes—they were the bluest of blue, ice blue, just like my father's.[63]

---

62 Siri Giancarlo was a thing of the past, terminated in my disgust over his uncaring delivery of the instructions that led me to Allen's house. Presently my directions were provided by Siri Victoria, a well-bred English lady who supplied her directions in the Queen's English and discouraged any tendency to drama. We got along well.

63 Thank you, I have heard of Oedipus. So what if I was maybe just a teensy weensy little bit looking for a father figure? In many ways my father was a prince—a prince who had round hips and wore his pants high up on his waist, but a prince nevertheless—so I could do worse.

Those eyes were like looking into spring water at the bottom of a Swiss mountain, refreshing, rejuvenating, and sparkling. They were so world-class, knock-out gorgeous that I bumped him instantly from an attraction rating of average to A++ and then some.

When George returned with my screwdriver—to my consternation, I never matured into adult drinks like Scotch and soda and martinis on the rocks with a twist— he invited me out to the gardens. Even at the end of October, the temperature was mild, and we strolled around comfortably without jackets, enjoying the sight of precisely trimmed hedges and the scent of roses. Somehow we got on the topic of the *Ripley's Believe it or Not* and I mentioned that one of my uncles had been in the 1929 edition as the youngest person at the time to attend college, enrolling at age ten.[64]

"Cool," said George, "I'm MENSA myself."

"What's MENSA?" I asked. George explained that it was a club for people with extremely high IQs. My first thought was, "You mean there is a club for smart people and I didn't make the cut? My whole life is based on a lie?" A slight exaggeration, admittedly, but not as much as you might think. Growing up, my mother roundly criticized

---

64   True story. At age six Arthur Garson (then Gottesman) was promoted to fourth grade after spending four months in third grade, He spent a week in fifth grade before moving on to sixth. (*See The Atlanta Journal*, October 5, 1924, p. 19.) In 1924 he entered Atlanta's Oglethorpe University at age ten and graduated at fourteen. My cousin, Tom, told me that his father was treated by his classmates as a sort of mascot instead of being bullied or mocked. Well done, Oglethorpe class of 1928.

my appearance (chubby), my sloth (partially true), and the weakness of my nature (patently untrue), but always said that I was one smart cookie. Much of my fragile ego rested on my brainpower, so to learn that even that wasn't top notch hurt. But I took the news like a soldier, because I was already smitten. Breathtaking eyes and a genius? What could possibly be wrong with that?

After our tour of the gardens, George and I went back inside and parted company, George to check on the bar and me to find Julie, both to thank her for including me as a guest and to inquire—subtly—about her brother. After several fruitless minutes wandering through small side rooms lining a long hallway, I found Julie seated in a pleasant room that in my youth would have been called the "music room" by reason of the baby grand piano located in the corner opposite Julie's chair.

"Well, hello!" I said, planting a kiss on Julie's cheek. "What a fun party and what a fantastic house. And the gardens!"

"You've been out there? Not too cold?" Julie asked.

"No, not at all. George showed me around. Your brother seems like a great guy." Subtle, right?

Is there a name for something that is more transparent than glass? If there is, that would be me. Naturally, Julie saw through me in an instant. And immediately went into high gear.

"Oh my God, you should go out with him! George is the best, even if I do say so about my own brother. He's been single for three years now, divorced from the psycho bitch from hell—good thing they didn't have any children—and it would be so cool if you two got together!"

"Wow," I said, "You really didn't like your ex-sister-in-law! Anyway, yeah, George seemed really nice, so let's see what happens."

Julie looked like she wanted to keep pushing it, but was distracted by some guests who wanted to thank her for the party on their way out. With a little wave, I scooted by and made my way to the dining room for some fortification by way of a quite delicious slice of chocolate cake with the perfect ratio of icing to cake—around one and a half to one—and coffee. Who should round the corner but George, looking like a man with a mission.

"There you are!" He said. "I've been looking all over. I have to go help Julie in a minute, but I was wondering, would you like to have dinner with me next Friday?"

Had Julie primed the pump so fast? If so, good work.

"Sure, I'd love to!" I said.

"Good," said George. "I'll get your number from Julie and we'll figure out what time and where." George waved and took off at a quick trot.

That couldn't have gone better if I'd planned it myself.

CHAPTER TWO

Guns N' Roses

Did I mention that I have never known a bad guy named George? Of the two Georges I had a thing for earlier in my life, both were smart, kind, and funny in just the kind of twisted way that is appealing, as well as cultured and good looking.[65] Even the several other Georges who were more casual acquaintances were all solid citizens. So when this latest George wanted to go out, the answer was an unqualified yes.

As I bid Julie goodnight a few minutes after accepting the date and thanked her for a lovely evening, her wink of encouragement added an additional bounce to my step.

---

65 You may be tempted to ask why I didn't end up with either of these Georges. Don't.

Maybe she had put in a good word for me, maybe not; in either case, a fun night out with her brother was on the horizon. I sailed back home, for once not minding the congestion that dogs Atlanta's highways even at 11:00 p.m.

The work week passed uneventfully, at least as uneventfully as the myriad mini crises that populate the days of a lawyer allow. On Wednesday, George and I texted back and forth, settling on 7:00 p.m. as the time he'd pick me up. Friday finally arrived, along with the ritual of "getting ready for the date." Happily, the usual frenzy surrounding wardrobe choice didn't occur, mainly because yours truly was in a pretty good place, feeling reasonably confident that a guy like George would find her attractive and interesting. Why not? For whatever reason, the snarky voices in my head were quiet, along with their discouraging refrain about being too fat, too uptight and not enough of a player (or the female equivalent). Good, and may their hiatus be extended.

George arrived promptly at 7:00 p.m. in a vintage red Mercedes that sported chrome wheels and a gear shift with a polished wooden knob. It was love at first sight. The car reminded me of the days of my youth and brought back memories of driving fast cars with sleek lines,[66]

---

66 Check 'em out:

Car #1: Burgundy Triumph Stag, eight-cylinder, matching hard top and convertible with roll bars.
Car #2: Silver Anniversary L-82 Corvette fastback, silver with silver interior, hard top and T-bars.
Car #3: Black Jaguar XJS, twelve-cylinder.

The first two manual transmissions, all fast as could be.

a cigarette dangling from my lips and hair blowing in the wind. Maybe everyone's life is non-linear, but my peaks and valleys have been nothing if not extreme.

At the time that I met George, my fifteen-year-old Lexus sedan was closing in on two hundred thousand miles. Quite a comedown from my beloved sports cars, but times had changed. Early on, my tenacity was admirable—even my first Volvo station wagons had manual transmissions. After a few years of juggling babies, dogs, and a stick shift, the dream faded and my first (and only) minivan came into my life. Still, to this day the sight of a snazzy sports car sends my heart racing.

"Hey, nice to see you again! George said, interrupting my trance. "I have been looking forward to this all week."

"Me, too. My week went pretty well except for the two days in the middle that sucked. How about you?"

We chatted in that vein for a while, nothing inspiring, just two people getting to know each other.

"You know, I never asked you where we are going for dinner."

George chuckled. "Yeah, I thought to myself, 'Either she's not a foodie or she is really distracted by something.'"

"You got me," I laughed. "My puppy won't leave my cat alone."

"How's the cat-dog battle working out?"

"Don't ask."

"Anyway," George said, "We're going to one of my favorite restaurants, La Grotta. Is that okay?"

"You like La Grotta, too? It's one of my favorite places for Italian and peace and quiet."

Located on Peachtree Road in Buckhead, the toniest area in Atlanta, La Grotta has been a staple of fine dining for decades. Courtesy of my gourmet mother, the owners, Sergio and Antonio, have been friends of the family since I was sixteen. Once, we even enjoyed Passover with Antonio, also the chef, at my parents' home. Needless to say, George's choice was welcome. If the date failed, at least excellent service and a delicious meal at a well-loved restaurant lay ahead.

As we arrived at the maître d' station, George said, "I get so sick of going to all the so-called hip places where the food is lousy and you can't hear yourself think."

Boy, were we on the same page, at least as far as the food scene was concerned. My children had heard me complain a thousand times about the same thing.

Standing next to the maître d' was Sergio's son, Christian. After a hug and a kiss, he seated us right away at a corner table, well aware of my preference for peace and quiet over visibility. Suitably impressed by my obvious familiarity with our host, George asked for a wine list while we scanned the menu.

"Oh great, they've got prosciutto melon," he said.

"I love that, too! Second only to bacon. If I was on death row and had to pick my last meal, it would definitely include bacon."

George nodded, adding that he would have to have chocolate somewhere in that meal.

Deep blue eyes and a lover of bacon and chocolate? I had to pinch myself hard to make sure I wasn't dreaming.[67]

After much deliberation, we ordered our meals: prosciutto melon for two to start, followed in his case by osso buco and in mine by a pounded veal chop with a side of spaghetti in a light marinara sauce. George turned out to be every bit the wine connoisseur I am not[68] as he ordered a bottle of red wine, a Barolo from the Piedmont region of Italy, to complement our main courses.

We chatted about nothing in particular for a bit, when I randomly asked, "So, what are you doing this weekend?" Not much of a loaded question in the ordinary course.

"I'm going to a rally for a congressman in North Georgia, a good friend of mine."

"Who's that?" I asked. "Maybe I've heard of him."

"Jeff Douglas, the Tea Party candidate for the Ellijay district."

Scrreeechhh. My mental brakes locked and the train almost jumped the tracks. My stomach jumped and suddenly food didn't seem like such a good idea.

---

67 No, I wasn't dreaming, and damn, that hurt.

68 God knows I should be a wine connoisseur. In high school, my mother took it into her head to serve dinner French-style every night. The main course was followed by salad, then cheese, then fruit, then a sweet. Big league wines were trotted out to accompany the cheese course in particular. Did I learn anything about wine? Nothing. Zero. Zilch. It was almost as if I made a concerted effort to resist the opportunity. I was extremely successful in that regard. I have no palate whatsoever and know just enough to recognize certain names I've heard…like Barolo.

"The Tea Party? Are you a fan?" I posed the question with some heat just as our prosciutto melon arrived, earning me a sideways glance from the waiter as he beat a hasty retreat from our little drama. Chicken.[69] The appetizer looked delicious. Maybe I could eat a morsel or two after all?

Picking up his fork, George said, "Oh sure, I'm a fan of the Tea Party from way back. I support the party's campaigns. Sometimes I even raise funds and help put rallies together."

The Tea Party? A member? Really? I had never met anyone who even admitted that they *knew* anyone who belonged to the Tea Party.

"So, I take it you like Sarah Palin?" Anyone who has read *Southern Vapors* knows how I feel about Sarah "All of 'em, any of 'em that have been in front of me over all these years" Palin.[70]

"Like her? I wish she was in the Vice President's office right this minute!"

Since the only positive thing about Ms. Palin was the material she provided for the funniest "Saturday Night Live" skit ever, I kept my mouth shut as I chewed my final bite of prosciutto—miraculous how that stomach ache had faded—and switched to the next obvious bone of contention: "How do you feel about guns?"

---

69   Not our food. Prosciutto = ham. Our waiter = chicken.

70   Famously, when interviewed in 2008 by Katie Couric, Sarah Palin was unable to name a single newspaper or magazine she read to inform her world view.

https://www.youtube.com/watch?v=xRkWebP2Q0Y

George said with perfect equanimity, "I used to hunt a lot as a kid, so I've been around guns forever. It's good I got comfortable with them early on, the way things are now."

"What do you mean?"

"You know, crime is everywhere, especially around here. I don't ever come inside the Perimeter without my handgun. It's not safe."

What? Most of my life had been spent near intown Atlanta or the closer suburbs. Sure, there were issues, but George made it sound like *The War of the Worlds*.[71]

A thought struck me. "So, when you say you never come inside the Perimeter without your gun, umm, aren't you inside the Perimeter now?"

"Yeah," said George. "As a matter of fact. I wouldn't do that for just anyone, 'ya know."

Nice compliment, and on the heels of it, our second course was served. The waiter deftly inserted my plate of pounded veal and pasta before me. Ah, the aroma! The taste! The vision! George eyed a robust platter of osso bucco with equal gusto. We ate slowly and silently, savoring every morsel. All thought was suspended in favor of the pure pleasure of the meal. Occasionally we looked at each other, enjoying the other's rapture over the food.

---

71 Whether you're a fan of the 1953 version or the 2005 version with Tom Cruise, you've got to admit that the story of the panic caused by the 1938 radio broadcast is cool. Apparently, some folks tuned in without hearing the beginning and assumed that the US really was being attacked by aliens. A small-scale panic ensued, with people loading up their possessions and taking to the highways. To their embarrassment, they soon discovered that you should never tune in to a show late.

That was a beautiful interlude, a moment of real mutuality. Why couldn't it last?

For one thing, moments like that never last. If they did, there would be nothing humdrum to make them stand out. In the more immediate sense, the moment didn't last because I didn't let it. Fork and knife on my plate, last bite washed away with a healthy swallow of wine, my brain rebooted directly to the last thing George had said before our food arrived, *ergo*, "Have gun, will travel" or words to that effect. I said, "So, you're inside the Perimeter now. Do you keep your gun in the glove compartment?" It made me twitch to think that the only thing in George's car between me and a handgun was a wood veneer dashboard. Beautiful, deep brown burled wood veneer, but still.

"No, I have a concealed carry permit. I'm wearing the gun."

No, that couldn't be right. I must have misheard. In my world, Jews don't have dates with guys who carry guns. Here's how it works for a Southern Jewish girl born in my day: you're born, you go to Sunday School, you get confirmed, you go to college, you maybe yes/maybe no go to graduate school, you go to work, you meet a guy, you get married, you have babies, you quit work, the babies get older, you go back to work, you get divorced, you go on a bunch of lousy dates, you meet another guy and you get married again. He has kids, you have kids, so you split holidays and everybody is happy or not happy. Somewhere in there, you go to Europe a few times, Israel at least once.[72] That's it. There are no guns in the picture, no guns at all. I personally had never seen a handgun and had only seen a shotgun up close and personal because as a kid, our Thursday night babysitter, Willie Mae, used to sit in front of the breakfast room window with a shotgun in her lap until my parents got home. True. Willie Mae also had famous sayings that she never tired of offering. One such was: "Meal time is a jolly time." As a food lover, I have to agree. And another: "A woman's hair is her crowning glory." That one was a puzzle. Was my hair still my crowning glory on a bad hair day?[73]

"George, what do you mean you're carrying a gun?"

"Tucked in the waistband of my pants in the back, under my jacket."

"Nah."

"Yeah."

"Nah."

"Yeah."

---

72 My family was the assimilated, *Driving Miss Daisy* kind of Jews. More traditional Jews travel in reverse: a few trips to Israel, at least one to Europe. Otherwise, we were all pretty much the same, except of course my family and others like us had Christmas trees and celebrated a secular form of Christmas. If memory serves, we even had an angel on top of the tree and a manger scene at its foot. No kidding. The presents were wrapped in paper from Bergdorf's (later Neiman's) and piled artistically around the tree. We had caviar and smoked salmon, and champagne for the adults, before we were allowed to open any presents. It was fun, in a stilted kind of way.

73 Willie Mae was quite a character. My grandfather met her cleaning elevators at night at his apartment building, one of two jobs she held down. He hired her to work at the family business, where she also held two jobs: one as an employee and the other running numbers for the local gambling crew. The consensus was that she made more money doing the latter.

"Really?'

"Really."

"Okay," I said, "but I don't believe you. We're done with dinner. I want to see this with my own eyes."

Our exchange may sound contentious, perhaps belligerent, but it didn't come off that way. George didn't seem to take offense at my incredulity. And while I was indeed incredulous, I wasn't attacking George. It was more as if I had a new species of insect under a microscope. George might have felt the same way. The likelihood that a gun toting Tea Party supporter had a rich history of dating Jews was slim to none. The safer bet was that I was the first Jewish woman George had dated or maybe even known. He was probably curious.

George paid our tab,[74] I thanked Christian for another lovely meal, and we exited to the parking lot. Handing the valet his ticket, George pulled me off to the side where no one was standing. While the area wasn't well lit, there was a full moon that night, so I had no trouble seeing as George turned around, flipped up the back of this jacket and showed me that yes, nestled against his back like some sort of mechanical slug, was a fat, glistening, black gun.

"Whoa Nelly! Is that thing loaded?"

"Of course it is, otherwise what's the point? Want to hold it?"

---

74 Must I really comment on this? Sigh. Yes, George paid the tab and I let him. That does not make me a traitor to the neo-feminist cause. It makes me a person on a date who is sick of treating who pays the check like it's a contest between the United States and North Korea. God, we have made some things so tiresome in the interest of progress.

Since holding a bag full of leeches tempted me more than holding that handgun, I swiftly replied, "No, you hang on to it, I'm good."

Right then the valet pulled up with George's car, so he flipped his jacket back down, smiled and said, "Missed your chance to feel me up!"

"Oh, ha, yeah, haha," I laughed weakly. "Next time."

Apparently, George missed the message that the whole Tea Party/gun thing really freaked me out. Truthfully, it might not be a deal breaker. Some married couples are polar opposites on the political spectrum, yet their marriages work just fine. We had a lot of other things in common, important things like bacon and chocolate, so maybe it was worth exploring matters further. Anyway, it was a two-way street, and maybe George had lost interest in me. Time would tell.

CHAPTER THREE

Surprise, Surprise!

George had not lost interest; quite the contrary. He called a couple of days later. "That was fun!" Skipping the preliminaries, he started out straightaway with, "Want to do it again?"

Yes, indeed, I wanted to see George again. I replied, "I had a good time, too, really good. Yeah, sure." Uncool, some would say, but when your feelings are split precisely down the middle about playing hard to get or playing it straight, my vote is to choose uncool. Several women friends who were once single and now happily united with their late-in-life soul mates[75] have sworn to me that the key to a good relationship is to have the man with his tongue hanging out. Others swear that "being yourself" is the ticket, and if that means admitting early on you like the guy, so be it.

Having experimented with both and failed miserably with the flirty, coy approach, I opt for the straightforward "what you see is what you get" style. How's that working for me, you ask? I plead the Fifth.

"How about Chinese this time?" George asked.

"Absolutely! I love Chinese food! I lived in Hong Kong for four and a half years, so I ate it all the time, and especially miss having Kung Pao chicken every week."

"Hong Kong, really?[76] What else are you hiding in that pretty little head of yours?" he asked.

"Oh, you know, the usual mixed bag," thinking, *like years in therapy, part of it on every psych med known to the Western world, a dysfunctional family, publishing a memoir about it all, that kind of stuff. Nothing out of the ordinary.*

But George didn't need to know all that, at least not yet.

75　Speaking of soul mates, did you know that seahorses mate for life, and when they travel they hold each other's tails? Should I be in the market for a well-heeled, middle-aged seahorse instead of a man?

Check out https://www.boredpanda.com/happy-animal-facts/ for more charming factoids about the animal kingdom.

76　At least he didn't say "Hong Kong, Japan! Wow, did you like the sushi?" You would be shocked (I hope) at how many times I have gotten that response when I mentioned living in Hong Kong. If you are not shocked, please put this book down and head to the nearest bookstore. Ask for a map of the world and tell them to charge it to me. It's the least I can do for international relations.

We set a date for Thursday night, just three days hence. George was definitely not in the habit of dating Jewish women, since he was obviously unaware that Jews of my era habitually eat Chinese food on Sunday night. Thursday nights are for whatever new fabulously chic, terminally-hip eatery has just opened to endless fanfare. The average person has no prayer of getting into that sort of place on Friday or Saturday night, but eager to try it sooner rather than later, can settle for a weeknight, not a weekend when the glitterati, such as they are, will be on the scene.

On Thursday, I had to go straight from work, so we met at the restaurant rather than him picking me up. Although unplanned, this had the added benefit of no gun vibe. The firearm situation still had me a little skittish, wondering what other surprises George might have in store for me. To be on the safe side, I had an out: my long-suffering friend, Nancy, was scheduled to call me promptly at 8:15 p.m. If I said the code phrase "The Kung Pao chicken didn't look good, so I ordered the Moo Shu pork instead" she would say she had a family emergency and needed me. By nature an open and honest person, law school taught me how and when to be devious, a good thing in navigating the modern dating landscape.

Arriving late, I hurried into the restaurant and spied George with his back to me in a booth near the front, a bright red shopping bag next to him on the floor

"Hey there!" I said, "You've been waiting?"

George, ever the gentleman, stood and ushered me into my side of the booth, "I haven't been here long."

For a moment, I just stared. Remember that statement that he wasn't typically good looking, but had great eyes? Not so true. He did have great eyes, but seeing him again, the rest of him looked really good as well. Maybe it was the whole package. He dressed beautifully. Hip but not too hip for his age. He wore a Robert Graham shirt, the patterns of the cuffs and the collar contrasting perfectly with the rest of the shirt, untucked and just the right length to be fashionable. His stone washed jeans fit him perfectly, not too loose and not too tight. George was also as suave and sophisticated a man as I had met for some time. When he stood to greet me, I could tell that it was second nature to him, ingrained. All very appealing to me.

The waiter arrived in a flash, took our drink orders—what a Chinese restaurant, sporting a fully stocked bar—and handed us each a menu. Scanning the menu just for fun, I ordered what I always order at Chinese restaurants: Kung Pao chicken and Mongolian beef. "Go big or go home" is the best motto when it comes to Chinese. George, also on board with the multiple dish-sharing concept, ordered Moo Shu pork and garlic green beans. Time would tell if we were a match romantically, but if food were the only criterion, we would already have set a wedding date.[77]

---

77 Family folklore has it that my maternal grandfather married my grandmother because she was a good eater. Since for most of her life she was what you might call zaftig—"full figured" for those of you still dodging my efforts to educate you in Yiddish—I could well believe the family tale. Wouldn't it be great if George had the same inclination toward healthy eaters? Probably not. Those days seem gone forever in a haze of media stereotyping, but I sure would bring them back if I could.

"So, how were the last couple of days?" I asked. "Working hard?"

"Fine, fine, nothing much going on," he answered.

But why was he looking sideways, at the breadbasket, over my shoulder, anywhere other than right at me? "Odd," I thought, doing a quick mental review to see if somehow I could have offended him. Nothing came to mind.

Then, as if he'd made a decision about something, George looked up at me and said, "But I did get you a present."

That was a curve ball, but presents are always welcome, especially when they are a surprise, so I exclaimed with genuine enthusiasm, "Wow, really? What on earth could it be?"

Picking the red shopping bag up from the floor and handing it to me, George said, "Look and see."

"Oh fun, thank you!" Inside the bag, tissue covered a book. Removing it, my delight faded, replaced by a large pit in my stomach and the feeling of heat rising all over my body, as if we were in a sauna. Was there any escape, like maybe a sudden stomach ache? I felt like I was going to throw up, as if I had just been assaulted by a fast acting case of debilitating vertigo. That wasn't far from the truth. Because the book from the bag was not just any book. It was my book, *Southern Vapors*, the memoir I had written not so very long ago. It was the book that put my guts on show for all to see, every wart, every emotional struggle, every imperfection visible.

Southern Vapors is not an embarrassment. Quite the contrary, the memoir is an abiding source of pride. The fact that I was able to write it, beginning while being treated for severe depression, publishing as I entered the road to recovery and going on to speak publicly about mental health as an advocate fills me with delight. That journey is a sacred part of my life, and nothing can diminish it.

By the same token…well, shit. The disclosures in the book are not, by any stretch of the imagination, second date material. Besides, our budding relationship, if you could call it that, was now all lopsided, maybe terminally so. By reading the book, George now knew everything about me, some of it quite alarming to the average person, yet I knew next to nothing about him. It was bad enough when I mentioned to Allen on a first date that I'd written a memoir and described its contents. At least it was all still somewhat abstract. He hadn't, after all, read the book, only heard about it. With the bright yellow cover and silhouette of a "fainting couch" staring at me from the cover in George's hand, it seemed that this time I had a reader on my hands .

Time to face the music. Looking George squarely in the eye, I asked, "How did you know I'd written a book?"

Oh, that MENSA mind, apparently inquisitive as well as intelligent—or maybe one is a prerequisite for the other.

"I Googled you."

"What made you do that?"

George said, "If someone interests me, I Google them."

Time for the obvious question: "Did you read it?"

George leaned a little closer, as if afraid someone would overhear our conversation. In the midst of my panic, I noted his cologne—nice scent. Old Spice? My father used

Old Spice. Was that a good sign? My mind wandered to anything and everything rather than focusing on the painful exchange undoubtedly ahead.

George said, "Yes, I read it. You don't seem like the kind of person you talk about in your book. I never would have guessed you had all those problems."

While it wasn't the first time someone had said that, the implications still got under my skin. How was a person with a history of depression and anxiety supposed to "seem?" Perhaps mismatched shoes, tangled hair, and a wild look in the eyes? Should a depressed person be incapable of articulate speech? Are we not a more enlightened a society by now?

It would have been easy to ascribe George's reaction to the whole Tea Party conservative ethos, but that would be facile. Based on my experience, our culture at every level is in fact not more enlightened, and George's reaction was no more or less than expected. As fast as I'd heated up, I cooled down. Then curiosity took over. Where was George going with this?

In as gentle a tone as possible I said, "It doesn't really work that way. You'd be amazed how many people out there have issues like I had and you'd never know it. A lot of people are trained to keep their problems hidden in public; at least I was."

George's expression was unreadable, but his body language showed tension.

"Does it freak you out?" I continued. "What's your reaction?"

"Honestly, I've never known anyone else who was so open about things like being depressed, being on medication, and stuff like that."

"Well, at least you're honest about being freaked out. That's a good start."

"Another thing," George said. "I've never known an author and I like the way you write. It sounds as if you're right there in the room talking to me. Do me a favor, Lynn, will you sign my copy?"

So that was it; laugh out loud. George wasn't sure if I was crazy, but on the off chance that I ever got famous, he wanted me to sign the book.

"Sure, hand it over."

Turning to the first blank page, I wrote, "To George, a fellow lover of chocolate and bacon. All the best, Lynn."

I never know what to write to people when they ask me for an autograph. Sometimes I'm clever when I have time to think, but off the cuff, it's not so easy.

Taking back the book, George set it down and put his hand over mine. "Look, I'm sorry if I offended you. The book was a lot to take in and it took me totally by surprise."

"Sure, I'm fine. Don't worry about it."

Throughout the rest of the meal, George did his best to charm me and it worked. We laughed, ate, drank, and generally had a good time. After a while, my earlier discomfort dissipated. George's concerted effort to get past what could have been a fatal glitch was touching and made me feel closer to him.

Over dessert—lychee ice cream, very creamy—George mentioned a trip the following Saturday to North Georgia, where he was meeting his friend, Jeff, of Tea Party fame. Shyly, George asked if I had any interest in going with him and bringing my puppy along. He said he would bring his dog, too, and we could take them on walks in the mountains. We would stay in another friend's mountain house for the night and come back the following day.

Third date road trip? Road trips are one of my favorite things, especially when someone else drives and dogs are involved. Road trips alone, like the visit to Allen, are a chore to be completed. Road trips with company are an adventure to be savored, as well as sustained by massive quantities of road trip food. The real question was whether we had attained enough critical mass for a road trip, particularly given the likelihood that sex would be part of the picture. For sure I was attracted to George, but sex with him already?

Hell yes! My "series of unfortunate events"[78] of the sexual kind left me primed for a sexual partner other than myself. "No big deal," I told myself, "I'm a modern woman. George and I have chemistry and I have no responsibilities other than work, a dog, and a cat."

---

78   Check out Lemony Snicket's *A Series of Unfortunate Events* collection even if you don't have kids. It's charming in a terrifyingly perverse sort of way, hence right up my alley. The author also wrote a book named *The Latke Who Couldn't Stop Screaming.* Get the picture? Oh yeah, for once I'll make it easy—latke = potato pancake.

The trip was a weekender, so that took care of work. Ace would be fine for a night—that's the great thing about cats, they are the definition of low maintenance. Augie was invited to the party, so there was nothing standing in the way. Why not take a chance? Why *not* live a little?

CHAPTER FOUR

Food, Glorious Food

"W hy George, I didn't take you for such a fast mover," I teased him. "Are you sure you're ready for me?"

"Ha. Don't spend a moment worrying about that." George arched a brow.[79]

Flirty boy. This was enjoyable. "Oh really? Then I'll take you at your word. Yes, let's do it, as long as you're sure about Augie. He can be a handful."

---

79 Arching just one brow is a facial display of sarcasm that I used to enjoy. For some reason, I can't do it anymore and that really annoys me. One less weapon in the defense system I've so carefully built to protect that fragile soul within. Thank God she doesn't need the armor as much as she used to.

"It'll be a blast. Augie will be fine with Bandit as company."

"Oh, that's your dog's name? Don't tell me he's named after the dog in 'Jonny Quest?'"

George was surprised. "Wait, are you kidding? Nobody ever figures that out!"

"It was my second favorite cartoon growing up. When Sunday school class changed to Saturdays, *Jonny Quest* was the light at the end of the tunnel. I counted the minutes to get home to a new episode."

"Well," he said, "we have a lot in common. I loved that show, too, and when I got a bulldog, he became 'Bandit.' The badass dog in the show."

Hey, this was really happening.

"Just out of curiosity what was your first favorite show?" he asked.

"That's the weird part. It was a love-hate thing for a show called 'Astro Boy.'"

"No," he said. "I can't believe this! That wasn't my favorite by a long shot, but I always watched it. Terrified, but I couldn't pull myself away from the TV."

My jaw was truly on the floor. Our feelings were the exact same about *Astro Boy*.[80] I'd never met another living soul who felt the same. This was a *big* sign from the

---

80 Does anybody else remember that in the original production of the series, no matter if they were saying, "It's chicken salad for lunch today," the characters literally shrieked every word in the most earsplitting, high-pitched voices? Scared the living daylights out of me as a kid. If you ever want to stress somebody out, send them a copy of any early episode of "Astro Boy." Blood pressure spike guaranteed.

universe. God up there winking at me, "Hey, dumbass, I got you what you wanted, now pay attention!"

At that moment, the waiter came by with the check. George grabbed it, and when asked whether he would let me contribute, he replied in a patently fake huff, "Don't insult me!" It had exactly the intended effect—backed me right off—and I made a mental note to borrow that nifty gambit.

"My, my, George," I said. "Now that I'm going on that road trip with you, what else are we gonna find in common?"

"Who knows? This is great. I have to say, I wasn't sure if I should ask you, but I'm glad I did!"

Now that we had that settled, my focus turned to the important question of road trip food. "What should I bring? What snacks do you want for the car? I'll take care of that." A woman I knew in my youth, practically a second mother, was a road trip-food-packing Hall of Famer who taught me everything to know about this niche cuisine. In the day, Helen gravitated to white bread, mayonnaise, and ham, with a side of chips and massive quantities of all kinds of cookies. Different times, different snacks. Nowadays road trip food means healthier choices like trail mix and fruit, but that is merely a matter of quality. Quantity was what really counted. The food checklist started in my head before George could answer.

"Nothing, just you."

Sweet, but typical guy. No matter, I'd figure out the food, particularly making sure we were well stocked. It was the least I could do, since George was taking care of lodging. We agreed that George would pick me and Augie up one week from Saturday at 6:00 a.m. to beat the traffic and arrive with the whole day open to us.

George added, "I'm helping Julie move this weekend, and with a really busy week coming up at work, don't expect to hear from me until then," he said.

"That's okay, thanks for the warning," I said (thinking, "wow, all that and considerate too!"). "How is Julie?"

"She's fine," George replied. "But, she's moving to a community with more activities to support people who are wheelchair bound. Her house is too much to handle by herself. Even though I live nearby, my work takes too much time to help."

And a family man?

As George paid the tab, I thought about it. "Maybe I can work with the whole Tea Party thing. George is such a good guy, so what if he's a bit conservative? It's not like I'm that political." Onward to the mountains! How exciting!

George wasn't the only one with a busy week ahead. Besides work, Augie had several training sessions scheduled. Housebreaking wasn't going too well, and accidents in George's friend's house were a distinct if unwelcome possibility. Moreover, Augie's trainer was the coolest guy ever. Alex[81] was born in Cuba, came to Miami as a teenager and after college set himself up in business in Atlanta and Miami as a dog trainer. In his off time, he does

---

81   Alex Valdivia; look him up. His YouTube video is incredible—make sure you watch the whole thing. Cesar who?

extreme sports and models for *Climbers Magazine.* Get the picture? Augie loved the training sessions and behaved ridiculously well for Alex, practically pooping on command. He would have gone in the toilet if Alex had asked, and flushed it after.

Add to that a big closing at work, and the week went fast. Suddenly it was Friday night. Daydreaming about the weekend as I packed, starting with how much fun it would be to drive the curvy mountain roads in George's car and…damn it! What about the food? Me? Forgetting about food? Impossible. Checking the time, I could still make it to Whole Foods before it closed. Augie in his crate, I locked the door behind me, and sped to the store.

Roaming the aisles, filling the cart from my checklist, I thought about the happy confluence of food and sex. Fruit? Check: Bananas, for sure, how much sexier can a fruit get? Apples and oranges, too. Crackers and a semi-hard(!) cheese like a gouda , savory on the tongue. Check. Bottled water. Check. Fruit juice? Yeah, why not? If we didn't drink it in the car, we could mix it with Vodka to sip in front of the fire. Just picturing the romantic setting made me smile. Charcuterie board? A little fancy for the car, but again, why not? Maybe just a little prosciutto and salami and dark rye; easier than making sandwiches. Snacks? Check: a few 80% cocoa dark chocolate bars, since nothing is sexier than dark chocolate, plus a bag of raw almonds and box of raisins. Check. Throw in a couple of yogurts? Sure. It was November, so no danger of them spoiling if we didn't eat them right away.

Standing in the checkout line, my eyes landed on one particular bar. Chocolate covered bacon? Now you're talking. What a nice surprise for George, my mutual lover of chocolate and bacon. Would two bars do? Better get four to be on the safe side.

Um, food obsession much? Guilty as charged. My therapy records all bear the notation "Binge Eating Disorder NOS."[82] Memories of food cravings go back as early as four years old, with candy bars lining the sofa next to me as I watched our black and white television. Those candy bars somehow provided a sense of safety in my otherwise uncertain world. For years, an obsession with food and body image ruled my life, unsurprisingly since both my mother and, unusually, my father placed an exaggerated importance on image. Rotund all of his life, my father was inordinately happy and proud when at eighty-eight years old, through age and infirmity, he finally got thin. At that point, it became a challenge for the rest of us to entice him to drink the food supplements that he so obviously needed.

And my mother? Good God. Can I just refer you to *Southern Vapors*, which is largely an effort to heal from her impact on my formative years? Sigh. Didn't think so. Okay. My mother was strong-willed, commanding, demanding, eternally critical, controlling, withholding, stunning, extremely bright and very, very angry much of the time. Hence the need for safety at age four. Hence the lack of self-confidence and the struggle to become an

---

82 "NOS" stands for "not otherwise specified."

independent, responsible and mature adult. For so much of my youth and adolescence, I was frozen in confusion, fear, self-doubt and hurt. My personal growth was delayed as a result.

Oddly, my mother was by far the more masculine of my parents in character, despite her extreme good looks. Beautiful, elegant, and imposing, yes. Feminine, no. That was confusing to me as a child, even more so as an adolescent and young woman. Who was the female role model? The male? So food became comfort, warmth, love, and even, in a not so subtle way, intertwined with sex. Food engages the senses, engorges them much like sex, and food wasn't confusing, at least not until it became an addiction to be fought, just like alcohol or drugs.

At present, my fight with food addiction is largely won, with minor and occasionally major skirmishes every so often. Not unmanageable any more. Thankfully, the journey to heal old wounds proceeds at much the same pace, allowing more time and energy for the pursuit of male companionship. Pursue George I would, laden with an arsenal of road trip goodies.

Arriving back at my apartment, everything lugged inside, Augie watched as I resumed packing. Wintertime in the mountains is pretty easy to plan. No matter how sexy you want to be, staying warm beats showing skin. In went my favorite blue and green plaid flannel shirt and a pair of thick jeans. Also a pair of attractive but comfortable shoes courtesy of Arche, my favorite purveyor for this type of footwear. Sexy clothes would have to be reserved for the bedroom. There I went hog wild. Black teddy with ivory lace accents. Since unlike Cher,[83] my age-challenged legs do not look fetching in a garter belt and sheers, a push up bra and thong to draw George's attention would have to do the trick. Throw in the Marilyn Monroe slipper pumps with the feathers? Yes, subliminal association with Marilyn couldn't be bad. Does an ankle bracelet work with the slippers? Personally, I don't care for them, but I have it on good authority—my friend Dora, who explores rather sultrier terrain than her more famous namesake[84]—some men are really turned on by ankle bracelets. Why I don't know, but let's not argue with success. Was George one of those men? Who knew? In fact, it was a mystery what turned George on. Tea Party. Ankle bracelet. Tea Party. Ankle bracelet. Hard to decide, but on balance, maybe not, although the least likely suspects are often the kinkiest. It would be interesting to see if that were true of George.

A bark reminded me that Augie needed to be fed, so I fetched a can of his food from the pantry. Much as I loved Hazel, this guy had really crept into my heart. He was the first hound dog I had ever owned, and after a

---

83 Did anyone else watch the 2017 Billboard Music Awards? Because seriously, what is Cher really made of? Whatever it is, there is zero overlap with my own gene pool. Jealousy aside though, I did feel badly for her when Gregg Allman died. Something about that pair always appealed to me—the visuals were just so interesting, like a saluki paired with a Shetland pony.

84 For those who did not suffer through "Teletubbies," "Blue's Clues," and "Dora the Explorer," Dora is the central character in a popular cartoon series that aired from 2000 to 2014.

few weeks, I was hooked, pure and simple. Stubborn, sweet, fast, strong, and handsome, that was Augie. His last session with Alex had gone well, so he should make a respectful houseguest, particularly since (according to George) his friend's house had a relatively large fenced area in the back.

Time for bed. A 6:00 a.m. departure time required that I wake up at 5:00 a.m. for hair and makeup and to put all of the perishables in the cooler. Despite my excitement, sleep came as soon as my head hit the pillow, a smile upon my lips.

CHAPTER FIVE

---✦---

Rocky Mountain High

Well, not exactly the Rockies, but still, mountains enough. The Blue Ridge Mountains are gently beautiful in their own right, as we noted when they first came into sight. George had picked me up at the crack of dawn. Now, dressed like a trucker in flannel and jeans, I was just awake enough to appreciate the surroundings. There is nothing quite like that color of blue that draws you toward those peaks, dark, velvety, and majestic in depth. Beaches appeal to me more than mountains, but the ruggedness, wildness and sheer scale of the hills can bring my senses alive. Here and there, a lone tree stood up like a hatpin, and we wondered how that could happen.

We stopped a couple of times to let Augie and Bandit stretch their legs and relieve themselves. Bandit was a cute little guy, and true to George's word, somewhat of a badass. Even though my hound towered over the bulldog, Bandit laid down the law the minute they met, and Augie submitted, rolling over on his back until Bandit gave him permission to get up. With a black ring around his eye and otherwise white all over, Bandit indeed had the look of an outlaw, but when he wagged his stubby little tail he was sweet as pie. Once Bandit established himself as the Alpha male, the two pooches became friends and shared the backseat companionably. George had borrowed a friend's SUV for the trip, so the two had plenty of room to roll around and lie down back there.

Without warning, hunger struck. "Time to break out the food,' I said. "You ready?"

George looked startled. "I just finished breakfast an hour ago."

Snorting, I replied, "What's that got to do with it? Road trips mean food."

"Go ahead, I'll just drive for a while."

Me: "Suit yourself, but you'll be sorry when you see what I've got."

Leaning over into the back seat, I pushed Bandit to one side and opened the cooler. Right on top were the bacon and chocolate bars, plus a bag of almonds.

No one really means it when they refuse food. I turned to George, "Put out your hand and let me give you something, but don't look until I say so."

After George's hand closed around the bar, I surreptitiously unwrapped mine. The scents of bacon and chocolate, each unmistakable, filled the car.

"What on earth is that?" George asked.

"Don't look, what do you think it smells like?"

"Well, chocolate for sure, and something else that smells really familiar."

"Keep trying," I said. "You're going to die when you guess it."

George sniffed the air or a few more seconds and then said, "I give up. It smells great, but what is it?"

"Bacon! Can you believe it? It's a bacon and chocolate bar, What could be better?"

George cracked up. "Where did you have to travel to find that?"

"Whole Foods, of course."

George said, "Do me a favor, open mine for me. I can't do it while I'm driving."

"Oh, now look who's ready to eat."

"Well," George said, "Since you're plying me with aphrodisiacs, who am I to turn them down?"

"Ha!" Bacon and chocolate as aphrodisiacs. Learn something new every day. Who wouldn't be turned on by them?

The bars were wrapped in that strange sticky foil that never seems to come off entirely, but after peeling away the last little bits, I handed a piece of a bar to George. He went to take a bite, but I grabbed his arm.

"We have to do this together," I said. "Right at the same time." Chocolate as orgasm. You can tell where this is going.

"Okay," said George, "One, Two, Three, Now!"

If you've ever watched the scene in *Harry Met Sally* when Sally goes into rapture in a coffee shop, that was the two of us after our first bite of the bars. "My God!" George uttered from somewhere deep in his chest, while I groaned with pleasure. "More! Now!" George demanded, and I handed him two more pieces, now a little sticky from the warmth of my hand. Downing both at once, George smiled: "You're definitely a witch, but a good witch."

"Yeah, but I'll still turn you into a frog if you piss me off."

The talk went that way the rest of the drive, turning from flirtatious sparring to comments on the beauty of our surroundings.

Before I knew it, we had turned into a community sheltered by elaborate wrought iron gates, fitting for the French countryside. Clearing the gates, we started to climb, ears popping the higher we went. After multiple twists and turns and just nearing the top, we turned into a short driveway that led to a garage angled toward what looked to be a very nice house. The house itself was the typical dark lumber used in luxury mountain homes, but because of the way it sat nestled in the trees, any sense of size or proportion was lost.

"Here we are," George said. He pushed the button to lift the SUV's rear door, got out and stretched for a minute, giving me a nice view of his hairy stomach where his shirt hiked up. Some women like their men hairless and smooth, but not me—the hairier the better. I need something to hold on to when I'm in the throes, dontcha know. George noticed me staring at his bare stomach and winked. Blushing, I looked away.

At times bold as brass, there are also times when the old southern girl shyness that lurks just behind the boldness appears. Right after setting myself up as hooker of the month, an overwhelming desire to retreat will like as not rush in. This was one of those times.

George held my eyes for a moment and then went around back to get our bags. I grabbed the dogs, putting their leashes on and taking them around the side of the house to look for the fenced area covered the moment. A perfect hangout for Augie and Bandit, the dog run had plenty of space cleared and the rest in bushes and trees. The leaves were falling and many of the tree limbs were bare, giving a nice long view of the property. Beyond the fence, the land sloped downward to meet a narrow creek at the bottom. Listening to the sound of the water, I hoped its soothing refrain would be the antidote to the crappy feeling that had just hit me. Being vulnerable in any way used to scare me to death and I still feared it to a degree. When George caught me staring at his body, I went back to that place for a moment.

Having gained a measure of self-awareness and resiliency over the years, I knew that my fearful state wouldn't last long. That knowledge, coupled with the fact that running water has an immediate calming effect on me, would turn my mood around. So it did, soothing my discomfort on the spot. I actually ended up congratulating myself.

Without resorting to uncharacteristic flirtation, I had succeeded in signaling to George that the game was on. Feeling relatively buoyant, I left the dogs to run and play and scurried back to help George with the groceries.

"What happened to you," he asked. "You were gone so long I thought you'd gotten lost! I've already taken the suitcases in and one load of groceries."

"Sorry, I was just looking at the creek down the hill. This place is so beautiful, let's explore it now."

"Do you want to do that, or do you want to go into town to look around and maybe grab a bite to eat?" George wasn't one of those guys who thought that just because we had come with groceries, we had to stay home and eat them.

"I'd love to go, just give me a sec to run in and use the bathroom." Glad to find that the embarrassment from earlier had worn off completely, I felt natural again with George.

A few steps led up to the back entry of the house, where I opened the screen door and entered. Some mountain house. A chef's kitchen, complete with top-of-the-line Thermador appliances, greeted my eyes. The kitchen was open to a great room with a soaring ceiling, supported by massive polished wooden beams. A giant stacked stone fireplace occupied one wall of the room, large enough to stand upright. Another wall had floor-to-ceiling windows looking out over the side of the mountain where woods flaunting the last of the fall colors extended as far as the eye could see. The furniture was a bit too boxy and traditional with obvious choices like overstuffed chairs and Indian-design rugs, but who could complain?[85]

A wooden staircase led up to the second floor and our presumed bedrooms. Curious to know the proposed sleeping arrangements, I followed the hall at the top of the stairs to the end, where a door stood open. Both our suitcases stood in what appeared to be a very well-appointed guest bedroom with an imposing four poster king size bed jutting from the near wall. Question answered. George wasn't playing courtly suitor—he assumed that I would sleep with him. Though a bit presumptuous, it was expected and wanted.

Opening the door to the bathroom, again I was knocked off my feet. All travertine marble and mahogany, with one of those showers that has jets coming out of every corner. The room had an oversized spa tub that sat in splendor in the corner. A mesh-screened cabinet boasted plush green towels rolled up with the edges perfectly aligned. The fixtures were Sherle Wagner, or something like it, and I figured several thousand dollars had been invested there alone.[86]

Of course, the facilities were perfect—shape, size, height, even a bidet for the ladies. That's a fixture I have never quite gotten the hang of, other than using the one

---

85 Who indeed? Hmm. If you twisted my arm, I could complain. Just a little. Does everybody have to follow the pack when it comes to interior design? Be brave. Give somebody other than the usual suspects a whirl.

86 For some unknown reason, folks who wouldn't take a step outside the norm in decorating elsewhere just kill it in the bathroom. Absolutely kill it. *Not* complaining.

at my mother's apartment to fill the dog's bowl with water. The bidet's adoption in America has always seemed slightly suspect to me, although it was undeniable that the elegant quartz-handled gizmo in this particular bathroom fit right in.

I checked my hair and makeup and went back downstairs to meet George at the car. Driving back down the mountain, he said, "I looked online and there are a couple of interesting things happening at the same venue. There'll be barbecue, too. What do you think?"

What indeed? Barbecue smoked out in the country over hickory? Great slabs of pork ribs slathered in deep red sauce, all tangy and sweet and gooey and messy.[87] What could be better?

"Yes, of course, that sounds great. What else is happening?"

"Well," George said, looking at me sideways. I was coming to know that look, and it didn't mean anything good. "Two things. One part is that there is a two-thirds-size replica of the Vietnam memorial from D.C. that travels around the country and happens to be here right now."

"That sounds great!" I'd never seen the original memorial, so the replica would be interesting.

"What's the other part?" I asked.

"Well, you don't have to go, but I really want to."

"But what is it?" I questioned. "How can I answer you if I don't even know what you're talking about?"

---

87 Sound like food and sex? Yep, that's me.

"Um, well um," George hemmed and hawed for a few seconds while I got curiouser and curiouser.[88] Finally he blurted, "It's a gun show."

A gun show. Shoulda seen that one coming, given George's outlook and the fact that there's probably a gun show every other weekend somewhere in the state of Georgia, but gun shows are so removed from my reality that it didn't even cross my mind.

George added, "Once I found out the gun show was here, I texted Jeff Douglas—my congressman friend—and he's going to be there. I could kill two birds with one stone by meeting him at the show. Then we'd have the rest of the weekend to ourselves. But I'd love it if you came with me."

Thinking on my feet for once, I replied, "Sorry, not my cup of tea."

George, ever quick on the uptake, immediately got the double entendre[89] and we both laughed. "Okay," he said, "no problem. We can eat lunch together and then split up while you look at the memorial and I go to the show to meet Jeff."

Which is exactly what we did. Lunch was every bit as good as my fantasy. Pork ribs with the meat falling off the bone. Brunswick Stew just how I like it, not too sweet and with plenty of corn. Coleslaw, which had slightly too much mayonnaise, but you can't have it all your way.

---

88 Lewis Carroll coined the phrase in *Alice in Wonderland*. Some people have all the wit.

89 C'mon, this one is a gimme. Not my cup of *tea*, as in Tea Party? Yes, I know you got it, just making sure.

After lunch, with my thirst quenched by copious glasses of iced tea and my stomach full of barbecue, we said goodbye with a quick kiss and a hug, George taking the opportunity to slide his hand up and down my bottom. Preview of things to come? Fine by me.

As expected, the memorial was interesting and moving in personal ways. As a kid when the Vietnam War started, then growing up as the news grew worse, the turmoil in our country seemed a normal part of life. Seeing the replica took me back to the days of college when I was fresh and young and oh so naïve. My freshman year roommate used to kid, with more than a hint of truth, that we were so dumb we didn't even know our own body parts. Sophomore year a girlfriend told us that when she had an orgasm, her boyfriend had to get a bucket and mop to clean up, because she gushed so much all over the floor. We believed her.

Engrossed in reading the names and dates of fallen soldiers, time passed quickly until my phone's vibration signaled a text from George to meet him at the front of the memorial. Hoping that he had left his Tea Party friend behind, I made my way across the grass, gave the replica one final look and, with some effort, returned to the present. George, indeed alone, relayed Jeff's apologies, which I accepted with a poker face. George probably knew that I was in fact relieved, but took it at face value.

By now it was 3:30 p.m., and I started to fret about the dogs. Had we left them too long? Was the gate well-locked? Did they need water?

As soon as we pulled in, I jumped out of the car and ran down to the fenced area, calling, "Hey Augie, are you okay?" Loud barking broke out. Both dogs were at the fence, pawing furiously in their efforts to get out. I leashed them and they dragged me up to the door of the house, where I gave them water and some of the charcuterie—fancy food for two very unfancy[90] dogs—but they had no objection. After gobbling the treats down they looked up expectantly, but I said, "No, guys, I'll feed you later; right now you stay in here and be good."

"George," I yelled, "Can you watch the dogs while I go upstairs to change?"

George slid open the door to the deck, where he was planted in an oversized Adirondack chair with a drink. "Sure, of course, why are you changing?"

"Oh,'" I said, with a sexy look, "Just going to slip into something more comfortable."

"Really," said George, arching an eyebrow to my considerable envy. "Don't keep me in suspense for long. Maybe I'll slow down on this Scotch."

"Good idea," I answered, toying provocatively with the buttons of my flannel shirt. It's hard to evoke Paris Hilton when you're dressed like Paul Bunyan, but one can try. George seemed to get the message.

---

90 Spellcheck doesn't believe that "unfancy" is a word, but Merriam-Webster gives it the nod, albeit in the bottom ten percent of look up popularity. Call me quirky—big stretch, I know—but I like using unpopular words. Sort of like rooting for the underdog.

Sashaying up the stairs, making sure to put an exaggerated sway in my step in case George was watching, I made a beeline to the bedroom for my suitcase. "Let's see," I muttered, "Teddy and cropped panties? Teddy and thong? Push up bra and thong under just a T-shirt? Or under a T-shirt and shorty shorts?" So hard to decide. Selections spread out on the bed, the common denominator was that all were filmy, gauzy, and thin. Sex kitten was the goal, yes, but it was more than a little cold outside. Better to cover up some and let George peel my clothes off rather than go out there half naked. That settled, the bra, no thong, a dramatically low-cut T-shirt, and shorty shorts did the trick. Let George have a nice surprise when the shorts came off and there was nothing underneath.

With a pounding heart and my nether regions beginning to throb, the walk downstairs and into the kitchen to make a short drink increased my anticipation. To help get me even more in the mood and to catch up with George's drinking, I added a touch more Vodka to the glass. As I poured, in came George, drink in hand. After orchestrating our seduction scene in my head, his sudden appearance put me off stride. My first thought was, could you please go back outside and let me make the entrance I'd planned? Instead, I managed to pivot and say, "Well hi there, I was going to come out and surprise you!" Twirling around slowly, I looked over my shoulder to gauge his reaction. "Do you like it?"

George grabbed me, pulling me backwards towards him so that my back was to his chest. He started nibbling on my neck and oh yes, that felt good. He gave me a little push and said, "Hold that thought, I'm going to take a shower." He bounded up the stairs, taking them two at a time.

A shower? Right now, just when we were about to get started? Did he want me to come join him? He hadn't said so, and besides, show me all the movies you want with steamy, sexy shower scenes where the woman looks magnificent and her makeup stays put without even the tiniest streak of mascara. That is such a joke. The first time I had sex in the shower I was in my teens, and the tile hurt my knees even then.[91] Imagine what those tiles—or in this case, marble blocks—would feel like now! No thanks. Even worse, imagine my limp hair and runny makeup. Not happening, no way. Better to settle in, wait from the

---

91   Not to mention the appearance of Willie Mae on the scene. Remember her? Rocking chair? Shotgun? No sooner had my boyfriend finished, we heard a knock on the dressing room door. We were in my parents' pool house in the shower in the "girls dressing room"—yeah, it was quite a pool house. I leapt out of the shower, wrapped myself in a towel and yelled, "Who is it?" Whereupon Willie Mae, who was still babysitting me at my tender age of seventeen, responded, "It's me, Willie Mae. You know you're not supposed to be out here! Y'all need to come back to the house or I'm gonna call Mrs. G.—"Mrs. G." as in "Mrs. Garson" as in my mother.

My boyfriend and I got dressed and came out of the dressing room, to be greeted by the sight of Willie Mae holding her shotgun. The sight was nothing new to me, but it understandably disturbed my soon-to-be ex-boyfriend. Willie Mae trailed behind us as we walked down the brick pathway back to the house, following us all the way through the house to the driveway where my boyfriend's car was parked. Her shotgun was pointed at the ground, but still. As he drove away, I waved goodbye and sighed, thinking "Thank you, Willie Mae: another one bites the dust." We went back inside and Willie Mae resumed her post in the rocking chair looking out the breakfast room window, shotgun in her lap.

nearest chair in a seductive position—oh and scoot my shorts lower on my hip—and fortify myself with an extra shot of Vodka in my drink. Wait for George to reappear, a cleaner if not more spontaneous person.

CHAPTER SIX

Next to Godliness, My Foot!

In no time at all, George marched back down the stairs, clad in nothing but a towel around his waist. He looked mighty fine, wet hair plastered to his head and matted on his chest.

Just as I opened my mouth to say something provocative, George strode up to me, grabbed my hand and pulled me toward the sliding door to the deck. "C'mon," he said, "This is gonna feel good."

Man of few words. "Okay," I thought, "I'm game."

Stumbling on the door sill as George dragged me behind him, his sense of urgency ignited a spark in me. "Yes!" I said, "Don't make me wait! I haven't wanted anyone like this for a long time."

Still silent, George pulled me toward him as he had done earlier, positioning me against his chest, backwards.

George held me tight as I started to turn, and this time he let me face him. "Ah," I said, "*this* is what I've been wanting." Closing my eyes and leaning back, I waited for the first delicious kiss, expecting a smorgasbord of pleasure. George pressed his lips against mine and I opened my mouth a little, waiting to feel his tongue. His pursed lips pressed hard against mine, while my mind raced with thoughts of tangled limbs, and I felt the welcome sensation of wetness between my thighs. Oh, right, that wasn't me, that was the liberal supply of Aloe Cadabra[92] I'd stuffed inside at an opportune moment.

George pressed his mouth against mine yet more firmly, lips pursed tightly together. This must be a new form of foreplay, but not overly arousing, like a guppy trying to kiss an oyster. Maybe a different angle? Tilting my head to one side, I sought George's lips with mine, teasing my tongue gently but firmly into his mouth, only to be met by the same resistance.

Pulling back, I inquired with all of the dispassion I could muster, "Hey, what's up?"

"What?" George responded with what sounded like genuine puzzlement.

"What?" I echoed.

"Is there something wrong?"

---

92 Who comes up with these names? Is there something about a sex lubricant that reminds you of pulling a rabbit out of a hat? Hmmm. Maybe so.

"Well, I don't know. I'm just trying to figure out why we're not wrapped around each other, with our tongues down each other's throats by now." Maybe not the most polished way to say it, but clear enough.

"Oh, I don't do that," George replied.

Thinking I must be missing something, I asked, "Don't do what?"

"I don't French kiss. It's dirty."

Couldn't have heard that right. This was a grown man, not a fifth grader. Not possible. "What are you talking about? What do you mean?"

Still relaxed, with his arm around me, George said, "I mean exactly what I said. Why do you think I went upstairs to take a shower?"

"I have no idea. I wondered about that."

"Do you have any idea how many germs there are on your arm? Forget about your tongue, just your arm? Not even your whole arm, just your forearm." He didn't seem to be kidding.

"Honestly, no, George, I never gave it any thought. I don't worry about stuff like that."

"Well, you should!" George said. "I always take a shower before and after sex. I can't imagine what I would feel like otherwise."

Talk about a buzz kill. Just my luck, I'd found the only male over twelve who thought French kissing was dirty. And that sex was something that required a pre-game, post-game, hose down. Was this a Tea Party thing?

Under the apparent assumption that our exchange settled the matter, George gave me an expectant look and drew me toward him, dropping his towel and expertly pulling down my shorty shorts with one hand while flipping me around with the other so my backside was once again pushed up against the front of his body. I stepped out of the shorts that had pooled around my ankles, aroused by the idea of some exciting foreplay in this somewhat unusual position. Foiled again. Apparently, foreplay of any description was not in George's playbook. Simultaneously massaging my hips and rubbing his erection against my rear, he seemed ready to head straight for the finish line. Whoa, this situation was getting away from me. Did I really want to keep going? Have sex with a man who thought the act itself was dirty? A man who apparently didn't believe in foreplay or facing each other or actually breathing on each other, lest he get contaminated by a host of germs?

To say no, it had to be now, but I was unsure. It took so long to find someone with the stars aligned and the attraction mutual, why waste it when I was this close? Yes, George had some strange practices, but having foregone sex for a while, maybe it would feel good anyway. Not to mention the awkwardness if I pulled back now. Once again, here I was, stuck in an isolated spot with a guy who, let's face it, I didn't know too well. Except that he was a gun-toting Tea Party card-carrying germaphobe. Best take a deep breath and plunge ahead.[93]

---

[93] Are you screaming, "NOOOOOOO!!!!! DON'T DO IT!" yet? No? Did you miss the day when they handed out intuition?

Decision made, I tried to relax and let my incipient state of arousal return. Think about a sexy movie you've seen recently, I thought. For some reason, *Gone Girl* popped into my head. No, not that one. The girlfriend pissed me off in the end. Goddammit, this was supposed to be the most instinctive thing in the world, next to sneezing. Why all this thinking? Okay, stop thinking. Let the sneezing begin.

All of a sudden, a hard push in the small of my back and a hand around my waist pulled my midsection upright. Thank God for yoga—I knew this position and automatically fell into a downward dog pose. George leaned over, holding me close, his erection nestled between my thighs. Again, a bit unusual but also interesting. The closeness of his body felt particularly intimate, and if he kept going this way, I'd be ready sooner than I thought.

Not that soon! Before I could blink, George was pushing at the entrance to my ———.[94] Wait just a minute, this me Tarzan you Jane thing was going too far. My state of arousal had barely begun; give a girl a minute to catch up. As I opened my mouth to speak, George thrust himself inside my ... I give up, my vagina.

---

94 What do you call your vagina at a time like this? "Vagina" is too clinical. I decided to research the matter and came upon, what else? http://eduncovered.com/50-great-names-for-vagina-2012-10-11, https://www.findnicknames.com/nicknames-for-vagina/, https://www.elitefitness.com/forum/chat-amp-conversation/238-names-vaginas-197006.html You gotta love the Internet. The thing is, I didn't like any of the other choices any better. I'm clearly not a prude or I wouldn't have written this book, but those words don't strike me as sexy in the least. Can someone please come up with a sexy, feminine, strong word for that part of a woman's anatomy? Don't you think it's about time?

There may be some mature women out there who are ready for action at the drop of a hat, but not me. So when George made his big move, it was not at all arousing, but thanks to my foresight with the Aloe Cadabra, at least it didn't hurt.

What it did was make me angry. George's failure to consider me—my needs, my wants, my desires—made me really angry. It made me angrier yet that, blissfully ignorant of my reaction, he just kept right on pumping, occasionally groaning with pleasure. Pleasure that was not being shared by me. I wanted to say something. I really did. Instead I froze, trapped between outspoken modern woman who was furious at being used like a plow horse,[95] and polite Southern belle who was too embarrassed to let him know that I was upset.

Feeling skeptical? I don't blame you. The embarrassment part is hard to believe, even for me. In my defense, please direct your attention to the late December 1962 issue of the *Saturday Evening Post*, published when I was nine years old. A trove of these magazines turned up in a small town in western Virginia that I was passing through a couple of years ago. The cover article of this particular issue caught my eye: "Today's Woman…" The text inside contained nuggets such as, "Women who ask for equality fight nature," and "Marriages don't work on a 50–50 basis."

---

95 It is an assumption on my part that female plow horses suffer indignities of this kind. For all I know, male plow horses are the Casanovas of the animal kingdom. If so, I apologize. There's money it in for any of you equine Latin lovers willing to come teach George a thing or two.

If you think that shit didn't get trapped somewhere in the psyches of all the impressionable little girls who grew up in the nineteen fifties and sixties, think again. Sure, ten years later everything we'd been taught came apart, and we jumped on that like white on rice. But for many of us, the other lessons didn't just evaporate. Early training co-exists with later influences,[96] and the outcome depends on the situation. In my encounter with George, they all came out sparring, which explains why I was paralyzed in the moment.

So I let George have his way, hoping that despite my anger, the sex would start to feel good at some point and at least there would be a victory in that. Which to my delight is exactly what happened! My body, accommodating to George's rhythm, began to relax and let go. Those little flashes that feel like mini-lightning shocks developed and grew, which reliably lead to a cascade of increasingly pleasurable jolts, culminating in a big mama power surge. Okay, George wasn't any kind of a kisser and had no clue how to treat a sexual partner, but this part was promising.

"Oh George," I groaned. "Oh yes, don't stop, that's so good."

---

96 Sometimes even the "later influences" carried mixed messages. A garden variety example: "In the sixties, not wanting to do something wasn't a good enough reason not to do it." Calhoun, Ada. *St. Marks is Dead—The Many Lives of America's Hippest Street*. New York, NY: W.W. Norton and Company, Inc., 2016, 138. That's an interesting motto to live by. And a double whammy as far as speaking out in a compromising situation such as mine with George.

Whereupon George stopped. Literally. On a dime. He gave one more deep thrust, came, released me, and collapsed back onto a chair.

Son of a bitch. Seriously? Yeah, seriously. Released from George's hold on my midsection, I sat down suddenly on the wooden floor. It was not only cold but also not particularly well sealed, promptly yielding a splinter that jabbed the back of my thigh. "Ow," I yelped, just as George popped out of the chair and took off sprinting to the door, singing airily, "Last one to the shower is a rotten egg!"

Now I knew I'd stepped into an alternate reality. This fool really meant what he said about cleaning off before and after sex. Did he have a scrub brush up there? Maybe a Brillo pad? One thing for sure, wild horses wouldn't get me in that shower with George, though truth be told, washing off the semen that was now dripping uncomfortably down my legs would have been nice. Personal comfort notwithstanding, not in this lifetime would I give George the impression that coital fluids were anything other than a normal aftermath of sex to be celebrated rather than washed off.[97] Screw George's antediluvian outlook and his lack of interest in my pleasure. There was more than one bathroom in the house, and the lovely downstairs powder room replete with oversized plush lavender hand towels would do nicely to sponge myself off. Holding my t-shirt

---

97 Did I mention that I came of age in the 1960s? Part of free love and free sex was that anything natural was good. That included dried semen. We were imbeciles.

and shorty shorts in front of my now ice-cold body—what a waste of provocative attire—I went inside to perform the needed ministrations.

First task, pull the splinter out of my thigh, luckily none the worse for wear. Medical needs addressed, I sponged off and dried myself with a fluffy warm towel. What a house—the towel bar was heated! Nice job. I put my clothes back on and went to see Augie. At least one male in the house had proper reverence for my feelings.

In response to "Hey boy, how you doing?" Augie got up on his hind legs, leaned against my shoulder and gave me his version of a hug. Aren't dogs the best? "You sweet boy, what have you done with Bandit?" Don't visit the sins of the fathers on their children is my motto, particularly if those children are dogs. As if on cue, Bandit came out from behind a sofa, wagging his little stub of a tail. For a moment, the world looked a little rosier.

Then George came down, fully dressed and wearing a scowl on his face to beat the band. "Ruh, roh," I thought, in Bandit's words. Now embarrassed by my scanty garb, I sidled behind the sofa and asked George, "What's up?" with as much good cheer as I could muster.

Apparently forced cheer wasn't enough, or maybe George was just spoiling for a fight. "Why didn't you come upstairs with me? Did I not satisfy you? Is that it?"

Oh Jesus, that old chestnut. Fragile male ego and all that. Is my dong big enough, long enough, hard enough, in every way good enough? At this moment, nothing could have been farther from my mind than stroking—yeah, I get the pun—George's ego; in my opinion, he should have been doing everything under the sun to placate *me*.

My pent-up frustration spilled over and the words tumbled out. "No, George, as a matter of fact you didn't. Did you really think that no foreplay and three minutes of you thrusting like a goat would satisfy me? Did you even think about me at all?"

George's face got darker, verging on apoplectic. "I wine you, dine you, bring you and your lousy dog up to this incredible house, and that's all you've got to say?"

Wait a minute. My what dog? My "lousy" dog? Oh no, my friend. Say anything you want to about me, but do not trash talk my dog. "What did you just say? What do you mean, 'my lousy dog?' As far as wining and dining me, if you want your money back, just ask!"

We were both yelling at this point, and in retrospect, I probably should have dialed it down a bit. Little as I knew George, his volatility was a complete wild card. But tuned up, I just stood there with my hands curled into fists and my face drawn into a scowl. George gave me a scathing look, turned on his heel and went upstairs. Fine with me; he was the last person I wanted to see right then.

Checking in with myself, I actually felt pretty good. A little cold in my hooker clothes, but all in all, pretty good. It wasn't every day that I let my anger rip. As a child, anger wasn't allowed, at least not at home. No exaggeration. An obedient student, I took that lesson to heart and carried it over to the world at large. Dating in college was problematic as a result, because every fight ended in a break up.

Since I had no idea how to be angry and work through it, it wasn't until I married that I learned that you could have a fight and come out the other end. To me that was the best thing since sliced bread. What a relief that my first argument with Wayne didn't have to culminate in divorce!

Recovering the jacket and shoes I'd left downstairs, I took Augie and Bandit out to pee. Five minutes later, mission accomplished and even the dogs beginning to shiver with cold, we were all ready to go back inside. Once I had refilled their bowl with fresh water, they ambled over and slurped side by side, inspiring the thought, "Ah, peace in the land."

A clatter on the stairs gave me a start. George was on his way down fully dressed and with suitcase in hand. Its hard sides banged against the bannisters, making the loud commotion that had startled me. Here was a surprise. He was ready to pack up and go back to Atlanta? That would be a fun ride.

As it turned out, there was bad news and good news. The good news: the car ride home would not be awkward after all. The bad news: the reason the ride would not be awkward was that I wouldn't be in the car.

Brushing past me, George grabbed Bandit's leash from my hand, and strode out the door, manhandled both dog and suitcase into the back seat, got in, started the engine and backed out of the driveway. All in the space of what, five seconds? It was hard to tell, because standing in the kitchen with my mouth open, my feet were rooted to the floor. By the time I came back to reality, George was out of the driveway and headed down the mountain. There was no possibility of catching up, but surely he would see me, come to his senses, turn the car around and come back for me? Wishful thinking. George's taillights—it was nighttime now—disappeared around a corner, and there I was, in the freezing air by myself on the top of a mountain, miles and miles from home. Oh, but wait, not quite, by myself. Augie was with me.

If you need a car service to pick you up at 8:00 p.m. on a Saturday night on top of a rural mountain with a forty-pound dog in tow, good luck. Uber was a joke, Lyft was a bigger joke, and it was too much to impose on a friend for a ride. A longtime customer of Buckhead Safety Cab in Atlanta, surely the dispatcher would remember me and show mercy. But no, she wasn't having any of it, partly because my loyalty in the last five years had dwindled in favor of the aforesaid Uber and Lyft. There are times when the new anonymous connectivity of convenience versus the old, slower, relationship-based culture really works against us, and right about then I felt really nostalgic for the old ways.

Light bulb: My mother had used a driving service for airport runs managed by the man who supervised the valets at her luxury high-rise. From the days when I used to help my mother make travel arrangements, Steve's name and number were still in my contact list from the days when I used to help my mother make travel arrangements. With shaking fingers I called his number and, miracle of miracles, he picked up.

"Uh Steve, hi, this is Lynn Garson. How are you doing?"

"Great," Steve replied. Former military man that he was, he got straight to the point. "Do you need a limo?"

"Well yeah, as a matter of fact, I need a ride right now. Do you have any drivers available?"

Thankfully, without pausing, Steve replied, "Yes, I've got a couple of guys who could drive now. What do you need, an airport run?"

Hooray! What a break; Steve had answered and someone was available. Now for the real test. "Um, well, that's the thing. It's not an airport run. I'm stuck in Ellijay on top of a mountain with my hound dog. I'd really like to get back to Atlanta tonight."

This time Steve did pause, a long pause. A couple of beats went by, and the only sound was his breathing.

Steve hadn't been any old kind of military. He was once a Navy Seal, explosives specialist, so he was pretty unflappable. That was a good thing, since my nerves couldn't take any more drama. Steve replied in a calm voice, but surprised me by what he said. "I used to have an old hound dog myself; best dog ever. I'd hate to leave you stranded, so sure, I can send someone, but it's gonna be expensive."

Wow, I might get off this lousy mountain because I owned a hound dog? Whatever it took, no argument from me. Since I would have emptied my life savings to get home, I told Steve that the money wouldn't be a problem.

Let's list the things that I could have bought for that car ride: four bottles of Dom Perignon; two weeknights in a cheap room in the Mark Hotel in Manhattan; an off-season, round-trip airline ticket from Atlanta to Paris; a year's membership to a good gym; one pair of Christian Louboutin heels, at the high end of the range. You get the idea. It hurt a bit, until I remembered how very much it meant to get home, and what it would feel like when the car pulled into my driveway. Even the drive, dark, cold, and lonely though it was, didn't bother me. In the words that had been passed down through generations in my family, "I had what to occupy my mind." [98] The driver deposited Augie and me in front of my door, relatively none the worse for the wear.

Does anyone think I heard from George again? No, I did not. Sadly, neither did my friendship with Julie continue to flourish for long. Her icy responses on the phone when I later called to say hello made it clear that she had consigned me to the "psycho bitch from hell" basket where George's other exes resided. Too bad, I really liked her.

---

98   One of my favorite quotes, based on some fun family history. In the 1930s, a woman named Miriam took a train from her home in Cincinnati to Atlanta to marry an eligible young man in my family. Miriam was viewed by our family as cheap at best and an outright hooker at worst. My paternal grandfather, Frank, was delegated the task of meeting Miriam at the station and putting her on the next train back home. He did so and, relieved that she didn't put up much of a fight, inquired of Miriam whether she might enjoy a magazine to read along the way. She refused, replying, "No thanks, I have what to occupy my mind." Add a thick Polish accent and you've got the picture.

On the whole, my takeaway was: listen to your gut, especially when it tells you the obvious. If you are a left-leaning centrist, do not expect your romantic match will be a Sarah Palin-loving, gun-toting, right-wing supporter of the Tea Party. The notion that love conquers all is mostly a myth, or at least a very risky bet. Lousy gambler that I am, I should have known that I'd lose that bet. Next time I'd be smarter.

INTERLUDE

Let's backtrack for a moment. A sampling of data and quotes from the afore-mentioned *Saturday Evening Post* article on the state of the American woman in the early 1960s shows the conditioning (indoctrination) my generation absorbed as children. By the time I turned sixteen in 1969, the "second wave" of the women's rights revolution was cresting in America.[99] Without the trailblazing revolutionaries who challenged the traditional role of women,[100] surely this book would never have been written. I would have married somebody named Isaac, had babies, kept house, done a little charity work, and called it a day. Look how much fun I had instead!

---

99   The first wave was the Suffragette Movement, which secured women the right to vote.

https://www.britannica.com/topic/womens-movement

100   "The problem lay buried, unspoken, for many years in the minds of American women. It was a strange stirring, a sense of dissatisfaction, a yearning that women suffered in the middle of the twentieth century in the United States. Each suburban wife struggled with it alone. As she made the beds, shopped for groceries, matched slipcover material, ate peanut butter sandwiches with her children, chauffeured Cub Scouts and Brownies, lay beside her husband at night—she was afraid to ask even of herself the silent question—'Is this all?'" Betty Friedan. *The Feminine Mystique*. New York, NY: Norton, 1963.

Saturday Evening Post Excerpts[101]

First, let's see in broad silhouette the composite woman in this research: She is thirty-five years old, happily married for fourteen years to one husband, and has slightly more than three years of high school education. She has two children and wants one more. Full-time housewife and mother, she is not employed outside the home.[102] Her average family income is about $7,000 a year and she spends slightly less than $7 a week on herself. She has no servants, no car of her own (although she has a driver's license); and she does not smoke, does not drink and does not lie about her age.[103]

***

Although womankind includes the divorcee, the childless wife, the working mother, and the old maid, they are not typical. These women concern sociologists because they are unusual in a society that is not geared for them.[104] This research was not a sociological examination of the extremes among the American women. It was an attempt to look at American women *in toto*.

---

101 All quoted excerpts appeared in the December 22, 1962 issue of *The Saturday Evening Post* in an article titled "American Woman."

102 Thirty percent of the married women in the study work outside of the home for an average of forty hours a week, but that was not significant enough to vary the composite.

103 The survey included more than 2,300 women throughout the U.S.—1,813 married/500 single; ages 18–60; more than two-thirds with family incomes between $3,000 and $10,000 per year/10 percent below $3,000/15 percent above $10,000; with formal education ranging from less than four years of grade school to those with PhD. degrees.

104 Ouch. As a doubly-stricken divorcee working mother, I would have been a real pariah.

***

A Midwest husband . . . was so angry when he found out that his wife had "talked to strangers" that he refused to speak to her for three days after her interview.

***

Repeatedly women told us, "The man should be Number One." A woman needs a husband to lean on as an Arizona mother told us, "Being subordinate to men is a part of being feminine." A New Jersey mother of three, who for ten years before her marriage was a competent career woman, explained, "A woman needs a master-slave relationship whether it's husband and wife, or boss-secretary. This shows she's needed and useful. Women who ask for equality with men are fighting nature; they wouldn't be happy if they had it. It's simply biological.

***

A mother of four spoke of her firstborn: "It was the one time in my life when everything was right. My husband and I walked down the hall to the hospital nursery together, and there he was, fine and dandy, and his daddy was proud."

***

Mrs. Jeannette Washington, a young District of Columbia schoolteacher, was typical. "Woman are easily satisfied," she told the researchers. "I'm happy with food to eat, clothes to wear, a little help with the housework now and then, and an occasional trip to break the monotony." In the Southwest a mother said, "The female doesn't really expect a lot from life. She's here as someone's keeper—her husband's and her children's."

PART FIVE

Richard

CHAPTER ONE

Dancing Queen

The holiday season came. Atlanta was stunning, the homes bedecked in wreathes and ivy, and lavish scenes on display in the front yards. The giant outdoor LED Christmas light balls were standouts; I'm like a crow when it comes to anything shiny. After my encounter with George, being dateless during a time of so many parties and festive events didn't bother me. My friend, Nancy, and I took a quick trip to New York to check out the holiday decorations and weren't they fabulous! Bergdorf's Christmas windows never fail to delight; that particular year they were populated with cascades of fur, velvet, and plaid. A couple of weeks later, my family met in Hilton

Head, South Carolina, the children coming from parts of the country ranging from New Orleans to Richmond to Kensington, Maryland. Reunited too infrequently, we all enjoyed each other tremendously and for the moment dating was far from my mind. By February, though, restlessness set in, and it was game on via the Internet. Renewing my memberships with the dating services—again—led to new photos and an updated profile—again—and with a deep breath, I stepped back into online dating. My response rate was still good and soon requests to meet were coming in at a reasonable clip.

After a couple of weeks, the cream rose to the top. A man named Richard seemed the most interesting choice on a number of fronts. He was age appropriate at sixty-four, seemed bright enough (retired advertising executive) and appeared well-traveled and sophisticated, listing Paris and London as favorite spots. Definitely worth a try.

Like many of my online suitors, Richard didn't waste time with preliminaries. After one phone call, we set up a dinner date at a locally owned eatery not far from my house, agreeing to meet at 7:00 p.m. one Thursday.

Following my habit of arriving fashionably late by fifteen minutes, I asked the hostess if there was a man waiting for me. She led me to a table where my first reaction was a world of thanks for better luck this time. Much better than Mark the Musician, tattered blind date of yesteryear. Richard was totally bald and carried it off well, with a short beard as a counterpoint. He was also tall and broad the way I like 'em, and initially appeared well-spoken, if a trifle too gregarious. Scratch that—*way* too gregarious. For after a little while, Richard started to join in the conversations at every table around us. He dispensed unsolicited advice about the restaurant and even shared less welcome personal commentary on topics ranging from world events to choice of menu items, noting, "You must be a big meat eater, you ordered the steak. Nice choice." The details have faded, but I do remember the woman at the next table saying, "Good luck," to me *sotto voce* when Richard and I departed. Not an auspicious beginning.

During that less than memorable dinner, we discovered one thing in common—we both liked to dance to rock 'n' roll. Naturally, we headed to that venerable Atlanta establishment, Johnny's Hideaway. During my law school days, Johnny's had been a place for good music with fellow students. It was also the rare joint that predominantly catered to older folks, and occasionally we laughed at the amusing spectacle of old women—younger than I am now—seeking partners. Nobody ever said the young aren't callous, and my group of friends was no exception.

Surprise, surprise. Turnabout is fair play, and Johnny's had become yet another hangout for the young, with only a smattering of older folks like Richard and me as the oddity. Since the music was still good and Richard was an energetic, if not visually appealing, dancer—he had much in common with the robot, C-3PO, of Star Wars fame—this part of the evening turned out to be a lot more entertaining than dinner. Soon after our arrival, a scantily clad woman appeared who had to be in her seventies, with long gray tresses tied up in a ponytail. Her big move was to bend over and swing the ponytail around her head like a grandmother version of Jennifer Lopez. Her gyrations were pretty cool if slightly bizarre to watch, and the woman's ability to grow such abundant, luxurious, and straight hair at her age was impressive. About the time that thought came to me, the ponytail went flying off and landed in a heap in the middle of the dance floor. More than anything, the wig looked like a dead gopher. The music continued but everyone on the floor stopped dancing to stare dumbly at the lifeless hank of hair in our midst. Mortified, poor "J-Lo" ran over, grabbed her hair and bolted out of the club.

The incident took the life out of the party, so we went back to the bar to finish our drinks, then headed out. At my car, Richard said that he had enjoyed the evening and would like to see me again, but he had a minor heart procedure scheduled for the next week. He would call me after the medical interruption. In response to my polite expression of concern, he assured me that it was no big deal and he would be up and about quickly.

On the way home, I mulled the evening over. Interested in Richard or not? Not particularly. Go out with him again? Probably. My mother used to say it was better to go out and be seen than to sit at home, always adding her mantra, "You never know who you might meet." [105] Not bad advice, especially during a dry spell. Despite being at loggerheads with my mother for much of my life, often

---

[105] My mother probably used the correct pronoun, "whom," but as many people can attest, I'm not my mother.

her little nuggets were right on the money. Such as: "Don't borrow trouble," for those occasions when I voiced concern over something out of my control that might happen in the future. Worrier that I am, that advice still comes in handy. Another: "Don't be a nurse or a purse." Cleverly put, and followed by any number of the single ladies of my mother's acquaintance, nodding their heads sagely when they said it while laughing heartily at the idea of squandering their time or fortunes in that manner. At the time I laughed with them, and tucked their collective wisdom away for a rainy day.

CHAPTER TWO

Be Still, My Beating Heart

After a week and a half went by with no sign of Rich- ard, I decided to do the neighborly thing and check up on how he was feeling after his heart procedure. Rich- ard answered the phone in a slightly breathy voice, but said he was fine. Even so, his driving was restricted, and he asked me to come and visit him one afternoon.

"Sure," I said, and asked for his address. His home was in a swanky section north of Atlanta. Occasional snob that I am, the location gave me some satisfaction. Sound familiar?

On the agreed upon afternoon, a 2:00 p.m. departure from work might help avoid rush hour. But there was no safe bet, and half an hour into the drive, my misjudgment of Atlanta traffic was apparent. Horrific on a good day and extra horrific on that one, turning around would have been the best choice. Then I thought about Richard waiting for a cheer-up visit and kept driving. An hour and a half later, I turned into the most cookie cutter, Stepford Wives,[106] nondescript community imaginable. It was a townhouse community, and when I say that everything looked the same, I mean *everything*. Every driveway, every front door, every garage door, and although it couldn't have been true, every tree and every bush. Nor was this community attractive in its uniformity. Most of the townhomes were faded stucco with water stains running down the walls. Gray is a vivid color compared to the predominant hue of this community. The homes were miniscule, with enclosed patios. A lone dog barked somewhere; otherwise, the silence was oppressive. Whatever might have been swanky about this part of Atlanta had cut a wide swath around this neighborhood.

Richard's equally unattractive domicile had even more water stains than most and featured a concrete pad in front of his garage. After parking, I walked up a short sidewalk and rang the doorbell. The door swung open and a pleasant-faced woman clad in a crisp white shirt and black jeans greeted me. "Hi, I'm Richard's sister, Lana. I've come to town to nurse him for a month while he recovers.

---

106 What a gift to pop culture that movie was; just the two words "Stepford Wives" sums up a look, a place, and a whole outlook on life that defined my generation in our rebellion.

Sure am glad I'm retired and have the time for it. So nice of you to come all the way up here." Lana talked on in this vein, eliminating the need for a reply, which turned out to be a good thing once she stepped aside to reveal Richard standing behind her leaning on a walker.

A nurse for a month? A walker? Richard's face was so pasty that he looked like he'd been rolling in flour. What was going on?

A few questions later it turned out that Richard's little procedure had been triple-bypass surgery. That explained his raspy voice and the reason he couldn't drive. Why had he minimized it? Maybe to avoid my predictable reaction—an unspoken impulse to get in the car and leave. Well, unspoken to everyone except my deceased mother, to whom I was telegraphing, "Hello, wherever you are, you know that 'Don't be a nurse or a purse' thing you used to say? I get it! I get it!" It didn't take an abundance of imagination to visualize her cheering me on and pointing at my car key.

How soon could I leave? Certainly not right away, contrary to my mother's voice echoing in my head, "No, it's good, go, go now!" Better to do the nicer thing—do a mitzvah[107] and stick around for a little while, then go.

---

107 Okay, I cheated a little on this one; now I'm making you learn Hebrew as well as Yiddish. On the plus side, your kids and grandkids will go crazy trying to figure out what you're talking about.

A "mitzvah" is a good deed or charitable act. The way my family used the word, it was one of those good deeds that adds maximum points to the scoreboard for the final reckoning. If you have the slightest concern about your place in the afterlife, you want to rack up as many mitzvot as possible on this side of the gate.

Game face on, I sat on a sofa opposite Richard. He gingerly transferred himself, with Lana's assistance, from his walker into a chair. Looking about, the place was seriously run down with rips in the curtains and holes in the carpet. Such a tiny place, it wouldn't have taken much to keep up, so what was the deal? Shades of Allen! What bad luck—twice!

Of course, it wasn't bad luck, and it wasn't a coincidence to encounter yet another guy in difficult circumstances. The problem was exactly what I postulated lo those many pages ago when I first described the kind of men who found me "visible." There had been a lot of older guys with good jobs in business, finance, real estate, you name it, who had lost those jobs in the Great Recession that began in 2008. Some of them hung on for a while, securing temporary jobs as consultants or short-term contract positions, but none of these jobs paid well or had any benefits. When the contract expired or consulting gig ended, they were told money was tight and they wouldn't be renewed. Left to live on whatever retirement savings they had, these dismissed souls struggled by, meagerly augmented by social security. Social security benefits were especially meager if they were under sixty-five and had to elect early withdrawal.

When the economy finally turned around, recovery was possible for those who were young enough to pick themselves up and re-enter the market. With a full-time job again and benefits, they could breathe a sigh of relief, promising themselves that they would sock more money away in their 401ks from now on. No big deal; just a temporary setback. Not so for the elder statesmen. Too late to reinvent themselves, they had aged out of the market and been supplanted. In many cases, their skill sets were obsolete. The six years between 2008 and 2014 were a lifetime in terms of technology advances affecting most soft industries. AutoCAD. Auto–what? Social media. What happened to advertising by mail? LinkedIn. Where's my Rolodex?

The kicker was that there, but for the Grace of God, would I have gone. In 2006, divorced, alone, and awaiting a settlement, I wondered if my daughter would visit me if I lived in a trailer. It was a legitimate question at the time. The settlement finally came and the threat of a trailer-home disappeared for the short term. Without a law degree to fall back on, it would have returned soon enough. Luckily, with a good resumé, I found jobs and made enough money to support myself in reasonable, if not lavish, style. One early job was as a contract lawyer with hourly wages and no benefits. The relief when another firm hired me as a full-time, salaried attorney with benefits was so strong, I will never forget it.

So yes, it was not only easy to relate, but also to feel compassion. Yet that didn't mean I wanted to date someone who had fallen as far down through the cracks as Richard.

Interrupting my internal summation of his life, Richard said, "I've been cooped up for what seems like forever. Do you mind going out?"

Apart from my desire to bolt, it probably wasn't a great idea to take someone in Richard's shape for a spin in my car. Nevertheless, compassion and kinship for Richard's experience won out. What the heck, a Starbucks was no more than a mile from his house, a good place to hang out for the least amount of time I could respectably spend without being overtly rude. Then, deposit him back home and split.[108]

"Okay," I said, "let's do it."

---

108 Do people say that any more to mean of "rapid departure, often leaving something unpleasant behind?" That is certainly what I meant.

CHAPTER THREE

And They All Fall Down

Sister Lana,[109] who had remained by Richard's side as he sat, hoisted Richard to his feet, placed the walker in front of him and opened the front door to bid us "adieu." She also bade me "Take good care of my big brother; he's the only brother I have!" "Yikes," I thought. "Driving Richard down the road seems like an even worse idea now. What if I have a wreck?" Too late, Richard was shuffling

---

109 My nanny, Ruth, took me to quite a few services at the A.M.E. church when I was young. As a result, I learned some Deep South Black etiquette, and "Sister Lana" rolls off my tongue as easily as "Aunt Sally." Don't know what the A.M.E. stands for? African Methodist Episcopal. I always wondered how you can be Methodist and Episcopalian at the same time, but I'm Jewish, so what do I know?

forward, albeit at a snail's pace, so I tried to slow my steps enough to stay at his side. As we walked (crawled), I racked my brains for something to say that would alleviate the awkwardness hanging in the air. Nothing came to mind, so we reached my car in silence and put his walker in the trunk. Richard needed help to get into the passenger seat. At least he was strong enough to buckle his own seat belt.

Tempted to say "How 'bout them Braves," I knew nothing about baseball, so that wouldn't work. Thankfully, Richard started in on his surgery, a topic that got us from his home to the Starbucks safely, praise be. Lifting the walker out of my trunk, I helped steady Richard in front of it. Then the fun began.

As Richard inched forward, his pants started to slide down in back. Oh no, I thought, please no. Oh yes. Richard kept walking forward and his pants kept sliding. Pretty soon, his butt crack showed. Gnawing my lip, I worried: Did Richard know? Could he feel it? Should I pull his pants up for him? What if they fell all the way down? They slipped a little bit more and just as I started to reach for him, Richard managed to snake a hand around his back and hitch one side up. Okay, better than nothing. That got us through the door and into the coffee shop with only half of Richard's withered ass on display.

Our conversation in the half hour or so we spent together was less than scintillating. Something about dating and women who expected men to pay for stuff—imagine that—and how miserable Richard was. There were a lot of sentences that started with "I want a woman who..."

and ended with "...but I can't find her." What a surprise. I mostly listened and nodded and as soon as possible, I said, "Well, I need to be getting back home to let my dog out/wash my hair/throw out the garbage/anything to get me out of here." Richard got up on his walker and we rewound the tape—me behind, Richard shuffling with his pants sliding down, me dithering about whether to pull them up.

Only, this go round things ended differently. Richard's pants slipped, then slipped a bit more and then all in a rush slid down his legs and landed in a puddle at his feet. To make things better? Worse? Funnier? Well, different, to say the least—Richard wore no underwear. He froze, I froze, and the mother shepherding her two adolescent daughters into Starbucks certainly froze. The daughters, on the other hand, who looked to be freshly minted cheerleaders with their ribbons and bows, stared with rapt attention at Richard's private parts. After one of those time-elastic moments, the mother shrieked at Richard, "Cover yourself! My God, what kind of pervert are you?" grabbed one girl in each hand and dragged them inside. The girls must have been part owl the way their heads swiveled on their necks to get a final look at Richard.

By this time, I could see the humor in the situation and cracked a smile as Richard and I pulled his pants up together, which at this point fazed me not at all. Unsurprisingly, the star of the show was not amused. We rode home in uncomfortable silence but for the radio. And my quickly suppressed outbursts of laughter. I tried, really tried, just couldn't hold it in.

Reaching Richard's driveway, I got out to open the trunk for his walker. Where there's a will there's a way, as they say. No sooner had the trunk popped up than Richard opened his car door, leapt out, and literally sprinted to his front door, holding up his pants as he ran. Following at a more decorous pace with his walker, we met just as he fumbled the door open. Muttering under his breath something that sounded like a very sarcastic, "Thanks a lot!" he fled inside.

No matter. After poking my head in to wave a cheery goodbye and say a quick "Nice to meet you!" to Lana, I headed for the hills, comforted by the knowledge that at least this episode had concluded without (a) mental anguish to one of my pets, (b) me getting stranded, or (c) the display of any handguns. Life was good.

INTERLUDE

Random Online Dating Message

GEN X GIRL: *I'm into art.*

GEN X GUY: *I am not into art but I have tats. Does that count?*

Random Online Dating Message

MAN: *Great Profile. Our match 0% so based on your logic. I have a question. Will you marry me? LOL. It was a great read and bacon rocks. There are some real freaks on here so beware. Even crazy women too. They said I work too much and they want to show me the life of medita-tion, yoga, vegan or whatever the heck it's called. It makes no difference how they look. No woman will ever get me to stop eating bacon and meat. I should have said yes and brought her a chicken fried rare prime rib cooked in bacon grease.*

Random Online Dating Message

MAN: *I have house by airport. You bring Klondikes. I have DVD.*

WOMAN: *What's a Klondike?* [110]

---

110 If you don't know what a Klondike bar is, run, don't walk, to the near-est grocery store, go to the regular ice cream section—not the fancy—and buy the Heath Bar version. It's the bomb, especially in a bowl with a crispy chocolate chip cookie thrown in.

PART SIX

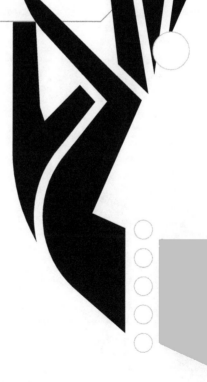

Zane

CHAPTER ONE

Rotten Peaches

Remember Bill Murray in the movie *Groundhog Day*, caught in a mind-numbing loop and condemned to repeat it until the end of time? His role certainly seemed apropos of my dating life. My brain said *"Basta,"*[111] but my DNA said, "You got this girl, this is what you were made for. Put yourself out there and the right guy will come along."

Guess who won? DNA trumps my brain every time when it comes to dating. Admittedly, another break was appealing after the debacle, brief as it was, that was Richard,

---

111 I like this because it sounds like "bastard"—my feelings exactly—but really just means "enough" in Italian.

but after a few months the mood struck again. And before you could say abracadabra,[112] along came Zane, with exactly the right bad boy name—an instant turn on—and exactly the right timing, showing up just at the right moment. We met unromantically in a grocery store, amidst the fall fruit of all things. Freaking fall fruit, it feels like such a betrayal, the last of the luscious peaches and nectarines gone, replaced by apples. Apples. Seriously? Yeah, the apple growers try to convince us that apples are the best thing since sliced bread, all these amazing varieties with enticing names like "Pink Lady," "Honeycrisp" and of all things, "Gala." Is there some part of an apple that reminds you of a gala? A ball gown and a man in a tuxedo, not an apple, remind me of a gala. Like Mel Brooks, I'd rather have a rotten nectarine than a ripe apple no matter how you dress it up.[113] Into October, the most devoted fruit hounds among us haunt the stores buying peaches and nectarines from any exotic locale. The farther away the better for the ever hopeful amongst us who cling to the belief that maybe in someplace like Chile they know how to produce peaches that don't taste like potatoes in the off season.

Standing there, staring morosely at the apple bins, someone tapped my shoulder. Turning around, a long-haired man, not young, not old, dark skinned and stocky

---

112   Not to be confused with Aloe Cadabra, although both entail a little magic.

113   In his epic recording *The Thousand Year Old Man*, Mel opined: "I'd rather eat a rotten nectarine than a fine plum." Amen.

spoke to me. He said, "I couldn't help but notice you staring at the apples, is there anything wrong with them? Something I should know?"

We started a conversation about my lust for summer fruit[114] and, before you know it, Zane and I had introduced ourselves and exchanged phone numbers. How easy was that? It had to be the universe busy at work fulfilling my destiny, no doubt about it.

On the heels of my last dating experience, it seemed best not to call Zane, so the first move was up to him. After a brief interval, he called and asked about going to dinner. Nice! He made the first move, and with a phone call not a text. We were off to a good start.

The restaurant Zane picked was on the other side of town, so I decided to forget being fashionably late and left in plenty of time in case of heavy traffic. Arriving before him, a table next to the window was perfect to flag him down when he came in. Presently, what did I spy with my little eye? Zane on a motorcycle, a Harley to be exact. Come on in here, you bad boy!

Have I mentioned before that I suffer from hippie nostalgia? Not in a minor way, more like a rabid, drooling dog. Guys with long shaggy hair who ride motorcycles beckon some baby boomers in the most irresistible ways. Right then and there, the stirrings of infatuation began.

---

114 Gotta admit it, some apples found their way into my basket, just climbed right in there. Any port in a storm, as my father used to say. When baked with cinnamon and a large box of raisins, they're not the worst food in the world.

Uh, oh. Infatuation for me is like a drug for addicts or alcohol for alcoholics. Something rises in my blood, attaches to a receptor, and a biological reaction takes place. Until I cycle through whatever process my altered chemistry dictates, I am lost to reality. Still I am aware of the risks involved in infatuation, so it's no big shock when a little voice in my head starts shouting, "Danger, danger, rocky reefs ahead, steer clear!"

Do I listen? Certainly not. What's the fun in that?

Zane sauntered into the restaurant wearing a black motorcycle jacket and carrying a helmet in his hand. His hair was windblown and he had the kind of tan that usually comes from months on a surfboard. I had trouble staying upright in my chair. Thought abandoned me.

"Hey, you look good," Zane said. Speech eluded me. I just sat and stared.

We ordered drinks and finally my tongue loosened. We talked about random topics as strangers do on a first date. Classic rock music played in the background, lots of Led Zeppelin and Pink Floyd, and soon we compared notes on our taste in music. Zane was born the same year as I was and had gone to a lot of rock 'n' roll concerts in the sixties that I'd missed. He rattled off the list of usual suspects—Janis Joplin, Hendrix, Jefferson Airplane, Crosby, Stills, Nash & Young (my personal faves), and The Doors[115]—to name a few.

---

115   All kidding aside, my serious, lifetime, forever crush is Jim Morrison. Mysterious, aloof, beautiful, drug addled—perhaps just addled—poetic, angelic, anti-heroic Jim Morrison. The man has been dead for decades and still draws crowds at his resting place in Paris. There's just something about him. Am I wrong?

When he got to The Rolling Stones, it was impossible to contain myself. Unlike me, Zane had actually attended some of the group's early performances. "Tell me what it was like!" I exclaimed, "I would kill to see them!"

"Instead of telling you, I have tickets to their farewell concert in New York[116] in a month and a half. Do you want to go with me to see them?"

Think of it. We had known each other for ten minutes and this man invited me to New York with him to see The Rolling Stones. Forget that we were strangers. The tickets had to be hundreds and hundreds of dollars. He was either (a) lonely beyond measure, (b) wealthy and devil-may-care, (c) crazy, or (d) some combination of the above.

Did I care? As the waiter arrived with our food—spicy wings for Zane, tuna tartare for me—I mulled that one over. Let's see, how much did I want to see The Rolling Stones live? How much did Hillary Clinton want to be the first female president of the United States?[117] How badly did Dorothy want to make it back home to Kansas? Besides, delay was not advisable, considering that Keith Richards should have been dead at least four times over and Jagger not far behind him.

Were there any little alarm bells going off? Any thoughts about danger or, at the very least, what quid pro quo would Zane expect?

---

116 One of many farewell concerts from the Stones as it turned out, but this was the first and at the time no one had any reason not to take them at their word.

117 Relax, this is not a political statement. It's a fact.

Sure, I'm not a complete idiot.[118] Just my usual M.O., blocking out the red flags in favor of a creeping infatuation. Some people develop world-class talents in chess playing or bodybuilding; others have devoted their energies, quite successfully in my case, to honing their skills in avoidance and denial. So, leaping out of my chair into Zane's arms with a big hug, I shouted, "Of course I'll go, I would love it!"

Just like that, plans fell into place to go to New York together to see The Rolling Stones. Reading up on it later that night, everyone referred to this as the concert in New York, but in fact it was two dates at the Prudential Center in Newark, New Jersey, December 13 and December 15. Fine with me; spend the weekend in Manhattan and take the train to Newark instead of staying in Newark the whole time. No offense, Newark. It's just, New York. Newark. New York. Newark. A bit of a no brainer. Sort of like Caviar. Carrot. Caviar. Carrot.

Marshaling what little sense that remained, we had two or three more dates before winging our way to New York. Nothing untoward happened except for the glad tidings that Zane had a dog, a big black Labrador. Always reassuring, it's hard to distrust a dog lover. There was also an opportunity to dispense a little sage advice, a welcome moment for any lawyer, no matter the context. Zane's dog, Jack, was suffering from the mange. Poor guy, Jack's elbows were practically eaten up with it and Zane

---

118 Debatable, but you can't fault me for sticking up for myself.

had tried every remedy to great cost and no avail. Courtesy of Willie Mae, gun-toting babysitter of my youth, the cure was well known to me. Apply a liberal coating of axle grease to the affected area, sit back and watch while your dog magically heals. My parents had owned two similarly afflicted yellow labs at one point, and while Willie Mae paid lip service to all of the gnashing of teeth, wringing of hands, and expensive unguents and ointments that she was asked to apply, she quietly brought in a container of axle grease. It took a long time for anybody to figure out why there were oily black marks all over the antique sofas and Oriental rugs, but by the time Willie Mae fessed up, the dogs were healed, and she was a heroine. Based on his reaction ("Hell no, I don't want axle grease all over my house!"), it was unclear that Zane would heed my advice, but both the memories of Willie Mae and the act of dispensing advice were enjoyable all the same.

One more thing our few dates taught me: Zane wouldn't let me ride on his motorcycle, which annoyed me no end, since I envisioned myself as an aging but still eternally hip Elizabeth Taylor careening around with Malcolm Forbes. Then again, his refusal probably was a good thing if I wanted to live to see the concert. Most of our time together was spent planning the trip, although to be honest, it was more me playing travel agent and Zane acting like what he was—a guy who had never been to New York City.

"Never?' I demanded when Zane dropped that little nugget.

"Never," he replied.

What do you say to that? As someone who had traveled abroad with my parents at age eight, visited grandparents in New York innumerable times before age eighteen, and later lived in New York as well as Paris and Hong Kong, I was a little nonplussed. Was there enough common ground between me and a man who in all of his fifty-nine years on this earth had never visited Manhattan, if for no other reason than to see what all the fuss was about?

Maybe not, but then again, we weren't getting married. The aim was to achieve simple companionability with Zane on the trip from Atlanta to New York on December 14th and back on December 16th, and more narrowly, to sit my ass down in a seat next to him in the Prudential Center in Newark, New Jersey on December 15th. Beyond that, we would have to see.

Putting a more positive spin on it, acting as Zane's guide to as much of New York City as we could see on Saturday before taking the train to New Jersey would be a lot of fun. To initiate him into the joys of Manhattan— the graffiti, the melting pot of people, the subway, Central Park, FAO Schwarz,[119] the Fifth Avenue shop windows decked out for Christmas, the chestnut vendors, even Penn Station—would be a bonus for us both.

---

119 It makes me sad to know that, should this book have (a) staying power, and (b) any of its readers be under age thirty, there will be those who don't know the miracle that was FAO Schwarz. Rent *Big*, starring Tom Hanks as a *very* young man. You'll see FAO Schwarz while enjoying a charming movie. If you don't think it's charming, please don't let me know—I prefer to believe that there are not people out there who are that jaded.

Finding a hotel took hours of research. Funky and interesting were my main requirements, and of course, not too expensive, since we would have separate rooms. When informing Zane I wanted my own room, he took it in stride and even insisted, over my objection, on paying for mine. Hmm. That was encouraging. A gentleman? Maybe.

The hotel of choice looked quirky and cool, The Blue Moon Hotel[120] located on Orchard Street on the Lower East Side across from the Tenement Museum. Our rooms were conveniently situated at the end of a hall, catty-corner to each other. If things went perfectly with Zane, it wouldn't be far to go. If not, I had my own room. What could be better?

Next on the checklist, make the plane reservations. As it worked out, our flights would arrive in New York on Friday in time for dinner and return to Atlanta at 9:30 p.m. on Sunday. Zane wanted to use points on Delta for his ticket, so my choice was Delta as well. Fair is fair, and with Zane paying for the concert and the hotel, this was the least I could do.

As December 14th approached, several friends began to insist on ensuring my safety. Despite my astonishing level of risk tolerance (a.k.a. death wish), I knew they were right, so I shared Zane's contact information with Nancy and my cousin, Jackie. I even sent them a photo of him

---

120   The Blue Moon Hotel was indeed quirky and I would stay there again, but it seems since to have gone "hostel," with many rooms set up like dormitories. Still, worth checking out for anyone who wants a low-key New York boutique hotel experience at reasonable rates.

so they could show it to the police if it came to that—call it the "trust in God, but tie up your camel" [121] approach. Rather than give Zane my address, I told him we'd meet at the airport since I'd be coming directly from work (not true). Ah, dating in the post-feminist era[122]—part business venture and part security risk, with romance bringing up the rear.

Wait. That doesn't sound right. Did I just say, with romance bringing up the rear? What happened to my knight in shining armor syndrome? And my willingness to hop into bed, if not at the drop of a hat, pretty close to it?

A little self-respect showing up, thank you very much.

---

121   According to the Annie Wright Psychotherapy website, this is an ancient phrase attributed to the prophet Mohammed. Why "Annie Wright Psychotherapy" is the first hit on Google for the quoted phrase remains one of life's unsolvable mysteries.

122   I have no idea what "post-feminist" means, but I heard it on TV the other day and it sounded catchy, although generally speaking, the whole "post" anything label annoys me. "Post-modern?" What is that? What's more modern than modern? I gave up on that one a long time ago.

CHAPTER TWO

New York! New York!

December 14th dawned a crisp and cold day in Atlanta, and according to The Weather Channel, clear but colder in New York. Luckily, there was no rain in the forecast at all, so no weather-related impediment would slow our explorations of the city.

We met at the gate in the Atlanta airport, Zane looking good in a pair of jeans that showcased an impressive butt for a guy his age. On our several dates, we had shared only a few chaste kisses and a quick grope or two, so Zane's wishes, desires, or expectations on the topic of sex were unknown. The sight of his well-shaped ass sparked my libido, engendering a hope that the trip would move our nascent relationship down the track. Maybe Zane, for all his bad boy looks, was shy, and some wild and wooly adventures in Manhattan would be just the thing to up his game.

We got on well as travel companions, perhaps a good omen. While not a sophisticated traveler, Zane flew regionally on business and quickly took on the role of ticket holder, clock watcher, and bag supervisor. Suited me fine; I turned my brain off in preparation for a fun weekend. With plenty of time before boarding, we headed to a nearby bar for a drink. That turned into two drinks, so when we eventually boarded the plane, I felt no pain at all. Zane took the window and I sat in the middle, the best spot for a fearful flyer.

Back in travel agent mode, I asked him what he was looking forward to doing in New York.

"Nothing really in particular," he said. "I just want to see a few things and then go to the concert."

"What things?" I asked. "Did you read anything about the city that interested you?" Planning the trip, I had suggested a few websites to learn about New York and its many offerings.

"To tell the truth, I got too busy and never read any of that stuff you sent me."

Wow. That level of incuriosity was a big surprise, though perhaps it shouldn't have been. He'd never been to New York in his whole life, so why would my suggestion of a few websites make him a convert? But. Even after a couple of relaxing drinks, something was bugging me. Oh yes. *That.* Already I wanted Zane to change, wanted him to be somebody else, a man interested in travel like me. The immortal words of Dr. Phil popped into my head: "How's that workin' for you?" In my experience, answers were limited to "not at all" and "never." Best to let go of the idea that Zane might magically morph into Christopher Columbus.

During this time, Zane sat quietly, nursing his drink. Feeling guilty, a renewed effort to engage Zane seemed a good idea. What more natural topic than his family? Oops. Maybe not. Zane had spoken little about them, and we passed much of the flight with him painting a picture of a wicked stepmother and brutish stepbrother. Sort of the male version of Cinderella. Wondering why that story had never been written, I mused on how screwed up Zane might be and what might be in store for the weekend. Too late: "In for a penny, in for a pound," as they say.

We landed and grabbed a cab into the city. Uber and Lyft (not to mention Via) had not yet gained the foothold they would soon enjoy. We arrived at the Blue Moon Hotel just before 8:00 p.m., with Zane grousing that he *never* ate so late and how were we going to find a restaurant? Please tell me the whole weekend wasn't going to be like that, was it? Me dragging him along like a clubfoot?

The hotel dissipated any incipient funk, with its eclectic charm and individuality. Trippy, there was no other way to describe it. Found furniture abounded, charmingly mismatched and frayed exactly the right way. Don't ask why that look is so appealing; I have no idea. It just pushes all the right buttons for me. Somehow it is linked to the very expected glamor of childhood, extremely elegant, perfectly coordinated, not overly matched, quite high design, and nothing edgy within miles. Edgy, as it turns out, makes up at least half of my psyche, generally setting up a conflict with my more routine half. Yet another dichotomy; is there any other way? In New York, I was all about the edge, within reason of course. Dangerous neighborhoods were off limits, but pretty much everything else was fair game.

We took the stairs to our rooms, which as promised, were catty-corner to each other. Opening his door, Zane gave me a sideways inscrutable look, though it was pretty easy to "scrute" it. Duh. In neon, his look said, "sex in the offing?" With an inscrutable look of my own, I made a big show about the quaintness of my room. It was, of course, quaint, but that was hardly the point. The point was, "Don't count on it, Buster." Not mean or angry, just fact. Zane shrugged his shoulders imperceptibly. Good; he got the message. Hmm. In the old days, I would have been on my knees by now, or at least pulling a thong out of the crack of my ass. It was gratifying that my outlook was evolving.

We agreed to wash up fast and meet in ten minutes, since Zane was so hungry. True to my word, in the hallway at 8:15 p.m., we shot out the door two minutes later. Without any plans, we made our way down Orchard Street, more of a power walk than a stroll, but Zane was in no mood to dawdle. After a few minutes, we checked out a Tex-Mex restaurant with an acceptably priced (for New York) menu posted on the window and an "A" for cleanliness, so we turned in. Again, not my preference, but I figured it was best to be reasonably conciliatory.

Perhaps driven by hunger, Zane was testy from the minute we sat down until the minute we got up. Nothing was good enough, nothing was served quickly enough, the food wasn't hot enough, the drinks weren't cold enough and everything was too expensive. It took a supreme effort not to get testy myself. Who was Zane to complain about *the* city, New York, the minute he set foot in it? For New York was my adopted city: my mother grew up there and I spent numerous Passovers at my grandparents' apartment at the San Remo on Central Park West, and my uncle and aunt and a number of cousins lived in the city—some still do. I even lived there myself for a brief but glorious period in the mid-eighties. I love Manhattan. There are two cities in America where you find an adventure around every corner—New York and New Orleans.[123]

Reminding myself that I was in New York on Zane's sufferance, his complaints rolled off me and I soothed him by stroking his arm and gazing soulfully into his eyes. It took a while, but it finally seemed to work. By the time we got the check, Zane seemed mollified, especially when I insisted on paying as a thank you for the trip.

Things were looking up. Would he like to go to The Bitter End, my favorite club in New York? Truthfully,

---

123 My college career was spent at Tulane University. Does that tell you anything?

The Bitter End was the only club I had the guts to enter by myself on my frequent trips to New York to visit whichever child happened to be living there during this period. Don't ask me why. The atmosphere just seemed low key and welcoming and I loved the music. Some of the acts at The Bitter End are going to be famous someday, no doubt about it. Besides, the nostalgia factor is off the charts—it's the last club standing from the sixties. Who can resist that?

Zane, that's who. He was tired. At 9:45 p.m. on his first Friday night in New York, he was tired. He wanted some shuteye before the big day tomorrow. Lord help me. It took every last ounce of patience I possessed.

"Okay," I said, "A good night's sleep sounds good to me, too. We're gonna do so much tomorrow; I can't wait!"

CHAPTER THREE

Santacon . . . Really?

Eager as I was to tour the city, we were up and out early. The best way to see New York is to wander aimlessly, and that's just what we did: to the upper East Side, a stroll in Central Park, cross to the West Side, Times Square, and finally Penn Station for our trip to Newark. On the Lower East Side, we watched an artist paint a contemporary scene on a sidewalk easel, took in a metal sculpture garden, and admired colorful graffiti courtesy of the 100 Gates Project.[124] On our way uptown, we took in Gramercy Park, where two well-groomed poodles

---

124   Art lovers, check it out. www.100gates.nyc.

frolicked, browsed a couple of electronics shops, and ate at a Greek-run coffee shop. Zane's mood had improved and he was almost jolly as he bit into his first New York bagel schmeared[125] with cream cheese and decked with real nova, not the Costco[126] version.

Leaving the coffee shop, it was almost 1:00 p.m. and we resumed our stroll at a slightly faster pace. Once again lucky enough to be in New York during the Christmas holiday season, at 58th Street and Fifth Avenue Bergdorf's holiday windows glittered with the latest fashions set against backgrounds of rhinestones and mounds of fake white snow. The vignettes could put a film set to shame, and I longed to pause in front of each one and savor the sights, even the narrow windows where handbags and shoes dangled and swung. But after just a moment at each display, Zane's low tolerance for "fluff" forced us to move on. Since a detour to A La Vieille Russie[127] was a must, I tore myself away from Bergdorf's.

Every time I'm in Manhattan, A La Vieille Russie greets me with treasures that White Russians brought

---

125   More Yiddish. Get with the program.

126   No diss to Costco, when I'm not in New York, I'm all about smoked salmon from Costco. That said, can someone please tell me how to separate the slices of salmon in a Costco package? There must be an instrument somewhere that can do it without hacking the lot into chunks, but whatever it is, it's not in my kitchen drawer.

127   The literal translation is "At the old Russia." For years the shop occupied an elegant space on Fifth Avenue at street level, but in November 2017 moved to the fourth floor at 745 Fifth Avenue. So worth the visit.

with them as they escaped the Russian Revolution.[128] Just by crossing the threshold, a sense of romance and nostalgia overtakes me. My Russian ancestors fled from *shtetls,*[129] not palaces and dachas, and they were lucky to get out with anything more than the clothes on their backs. Still, artifacts from that time and place intrigue me and I seek them out when and where I can.

At the shop, a somber gentleman buzzed us in, with Zane looking doubtful—understandable on every level— the shop is imposing and even intimidating, plus Zane's interest in the items sold there had to be nil.

But no! As luck had it, the shop had just hosted an exhibition of watches and watchmaking and still had several items on display. Zane had a passion for watches and perked right up, questioning a salesperson at length about the mechanics and movements of several of the pieces. Meanwhile, I happily browsed among old sterling, real Fabergé objects, including two Imperial Easter Eggs, a great deal of antique porcelain, and cases of magnificent jewelry.

After a half hour, we reluctantly left and continued in the direction of Central Park to take in some sunshine and nature New York-style. At the corner of Central Park South and Fifth Avenue, we saw a group of Santa

---

128   If this is no longer the source of their wares, I don't want to know it; I'd rather pretend that there is still some glamour left in the world.

129   "Shtetl" is the Yiddish(!) word for the small villages in Russia and Poland where the Jews once lived, made famous in earlier times by the Broadway musical, *Fiddler on the Roof.*

Claus revelers who turned out to be kids in their twenties dressed like Santa down to their beards, and they were clearly toasted. A female Santa asked us to take a picture of their group, and they took a few of us on my phone in return. As an afterthought, Zane asked them whether they were going to an early Christmas party.

"Oh no," a tall thin Santa responded, "this is Santacon."

"Santa, what?" Zane asked.

"Santacon," all five chimed in. "It's a pub crawl where everybody dresses like the jolly old Dude."

"Oh, that sounds like fun," I said. "Is it all over the city?"

"Uh-huh," tall thin Santa said. "It's particular bars, but right now everybody seems to be gathering over by Penn Station."

"Oh?" I replied, looking at Zane. "That's where we're headed. We're catching a 4:00 p.m. train to Newark."

"Good luck with that," the skinny Santa said. "It's wall-to-wall people down that way."

By this time, it was 2:00 p.m. and we needed to get going to have any chance of making a 4:00 p.m. train. Grabbing Zane's hand, I shouted, "Guys, thanks for the tip!" over my shoulder and started hurrying down Sixth Avenue. Thinking we might still take in Times Square on the way to the train station, I steered us onto 47th Street on the way to Seventh Avenue. Big mistake. Colossal, world class mistake.

Crowds of Santas clogged the sidewalks. Everywhere you looked there were Santas—short, tall, fat, Black,

White, Asian, male, female, you name it—but they all had one thing in common. They were drunk. My God, were they drunk. Falling down, blind, staggering drunk.[130] Closer to Seventh Avenue, the crowds thickened even more. The nearer we got, the drunker the Santas were. At the corner of 47th and Seventh, we tried to turn left and head downtown, but failed. If you've ever been to the Bacchus Parade in New Orleans during Mardi Gras, you have an idea of the crowd size. It was wall-to-wall revelry, and it was immobile. You couldn't move or turn, and it was easy to get separated. Suddenly the crowd lurched. Next thing I knew, I was up in the air with my back mashed against the side of a shop window and my face buried in Zane's crotch, unable to breathe. Swiveling my head with difficulty, I saw that Zane had pinioned me and stood spread-eagled with his arms extended in the air. His face wore the oddest expression.

"Zane? Zane? Hello, Earth to Zane!"

No response. Panic began to flare inside me. Everything got a little sharper and brighter. "Hey!" I yelled, trying to struggle loose. After what seemed like minutes, Zane's eyes cleared and he pushed back against a momentarily thinning crowd, giving me space to step back from the wall and take a deep breath.

Still amped up, I snapped, "Why did you do that?"

---

130 In case you think this is literary license, Huffington Post's description of Santacon was: "Nothing says Christmas like thousands of drunk Santas roaming New York streets. This, friends, is Santacon."

Looking smug, Zane replied, "I learned that little trick from a Navy Seal handbook. Any time you're in a mob, you should try to get up high."

Right. This was hardly the mountains of Afghanistan, unless the high-rise buildings counted for elevation.

"You never told me you were in the Seals. When was that?"

"Oh no," he said. "I wasn't *in* the Seals, I'm just obsessed with them. I have a whole collection of patches, t-shirts, posters, hunting decals, stickers, knives—whatever I can lay my hands on. Particularly knives. I have a big collection of those. The Bayonet knives are the best."

Knives? *Bayonet knives?* Another date with a penchant for weapons? First guns, now knives. Thank you, Karma. I must really have sucked in a previous life. So who was this guy, really? Maybe my spontaneous, oh so cavalier acceptance of Zane's invitation hadn't been very wise after all. For a moment there he had actually looked unhinged.

Totally creeped out and laying on a heavy dose of Southern charm to mask it, I exclaimed, "Oh how interesting! Let's talk about that once we get to the train, but for now, let's get a move on."

Something turned cold in Zane's eyes. Apparently, the Southern charm gambit hadn't worked and Zane had caught a glimpse of my dismay. Despite the warm afternoon sun and the renewed press of the crowd, there was a definite chill in the air.

No time to worry about that now. We really had to get to the station.

Every step of the way through the crowd was a struggle. It became so taxing that we had to go down to Eighth Avenue and walk back up to the far side of Penn Station. With barely enough time to buy our tickets and get on the train, we somehow made it. Collapsing in our seats, I tried to mend fences with Zane. With a lot of enthusiasm, most of it genuine, I looked gratefully into his eyes and said, "I'm so looking forward to this concert. Thank you for everything!"

Zane grunted and said, "Excuse me, I need to go make a phone call."

What? Saturday night on the train to see The Rolling Stones, and all of a sudden he had to make a phone call? But no explanation was forthcoming when Zane returned to our seats right before the train pulled into Newark. As we got to the waiting room on our way out of the station, he said curtly, "Stay here for a minute. I have to make another call."

"Okay," I said with false cheerfulness, and sat down on a wooden bench.

And sat. And sat. The bench was starting to feel uncomfortably hard and the big wall clock facing me seemed to move at a snail's pace.

Then a quiet, small thought crept into my mind. Was this guy ditching me because I hadn't been enthusiastic enough about him being a pseudo Navy Seal? Seriously? Nah, couldn't be. He would be back any minute. Minutes passed, and the small thought got louder. Could it be? Literally at the gates of one of The Rolling Stones' last concerts ever? Nah.

More time passed, and, unbelievably, it seemed I had been abandoned in the Newark train station. Not only that, but like an idiot I hadn't brought my wallet. By dint of marginally intelligent planning, I had my phone, even the charger, and a return train ticket, but no pesky cash or credit cards on me. So bulky, too many bulges in my skinny jeans. Far better to be at the mercy of a virtual stranger, don't you think? Taking a deep breath, I called Liz, one of my oldest and best friends, who has lived in New York forever and was certain to bail me out if only she could be reached.

Praise be, she picked up on the second ring.

"Liz? Is that you?" My voice shook and my fingers were white from clutching the phone.

"Yes, it's me. You sound awful! Are you okay?"

"No, not exactly. I'm stranded at the Newark train station with no cash. My idiot date has ditched me. If I make it back to the city, can you come get me?"

Liz replied in a voice one would use with a small child, "Yes of course. Just tell me when and…"

At that moment, Zane pushed through the door to the station and headed my way.

"Thanks, Liz," I interrupted her. "But guess who's just come back?"

"Let's hope that's a good thing," she said. "Call me if it goes south."

"Will do. Wish me luck."

I smiled dazzlingly at Zane: "Welcome back! What was all that about?"

Zane said, "A real estate deal. There were some last-minute issues."

On Saturday night at 6:30 p.m.? Whatever you say.

I dutifully tagged along with Zane and a blast of chill air hit us as we exited the station. Walking towards Prudential Center with the growing crowd, we made our way around barriers and cut through parking lots until we finally arrived at the venue.

"Should we buy t-shirts now or wait 'til after?" I asked.

"Let's wait," Zane said. "I'm ready to get out of the cold."

"Okay, maybe we'll get something to eat. You hungry?"

"Yeah, really hungry now that I think about it."

"Okay," I said, "my treat."

Famous last words. Dinner at Prudential Center cost about the same as a meal for two at one of the better restaurants in Atlanta, minus alcohol. Three Kosher hot dogs—hold the chili—one mammoth diet coke, two draft beers, one large order of fries, a large popcorn and a bag of M&Ms, all for a mere one hundred and twenty-three dollars plus tax. That hurt. Then again, Zane had spent a fortune on the tickets, although he hadn't told me the exact amount.

He corrected that oversight soon after we went into the arena and found our seats. Our tickets were on the floor, normally a good thing. The problem was that the floor was huge and the floor seats went way back. The arena felt like an airplane hangar, and our seats were so far back, they were the equivalent of a nosebleed section without the angle. Thankfully, we had both brought binoculars, but at my height, it was unclear how helpful they would be.

When Zane saw where we were seated, he lost his cool, "Fuck! I paid twelve hundred dollars for these tickets! I can barely see the stage!"

"Whoa, you paid six hundred dollars each for these tickets? I had no idea they were that expensive." I figured that the tickets were pricey, but not that much.

"Have you been under a rock? This is one of the hottest shows ever. I paid twelve hundred dollars *each*. And this is all I got for my money!"

"Zane! I had no idea!" Twelve hundred dollars a ticket? Never would I pay that much money to see a show, no matter who or what it was. Shocked by the thought of six hundred dollars, twelve hundred dollars knocked me over.[131] "Thank you, Zane. I really do appreciate it."

The thanks were genuine. It was hard to believe Zane had spent that much money on me. Best I could tell, he was not a wealthy guy, just an avid music fan willing to make some sacrifices for the Stones' last tour. Presumably there were others he could have invited to join him.

"Yeah," he replied. "I hope it's worth it."

What a gentleman. It was unclear whether he meant the show or me, but in the general spirit of gratitude and excitement, it was the concert that mattered.

---

131   Remember, this all happened before *Hamilton* came to Broadway. To give you my perspective, I still haven't seen it; call me stingy, but that eight hundred dollars feels better in my pocket or on my feet. Broadway shows are fleeting, but shoes last forever if you take good care of them.

CHAPTER FOUR

Gimme Shelter

Though we arrived at the arena early, time passed quickly until the show began. When the lights finally dimmed, the crowd went wild. Everyone jumped up hoping to see Mick Jagger and equally Keith Richards, gnarly old tree trunk that he is.[132] For me, no such luck. Most everyone topped me by at least six inches and there was a leviathan two rows up who could have found work as a sumo wrestler. Never mind, who expects to see the

---

132 You gotta give credit where credit is due—Richards and Yggdrasil could go head to head in a contest for gnarliness and Yggdrasil would probably lose. I will give a book to the first ten people under thirty who can identify Yggdrasil without looking it up. I'm not sure what that says about the winners, but at least they'll get a free book out of the deal.

stage, anyway? Whipping out the binoculars, a small figure up there seemed to be gamboling and prancing about.
He resembled Mick, but I couldn't be sure. His voice, in
fine form, was definitely recognizable, so that clinched the
deal. Was that guy with what looked like a long stick in
his hand Keith Richards? Yes, it was! How cool was this?

Glancing over at Zane, he had his phone up videoing
the show, looking pretty serious about it. Was he excited
and having a good time? It was difficult to tell. Back on
stage, the other talent on the bill with the Stones—Gary
Clark Jr., John Mayer, the Black Keys, Springsteen, and
Lady Gaga—were equally thrilling. My neighbor to the
left and the couple sitting in front of me shared my excitement. We had all talked (except Zane) before the concert
started and now we were all dancing together, high-fiv-
ing, and generally having a ball. Forty-five minutes into
the show, Lady Gaga came on to the opening notes of
"Gimme Shelter." I could have died and gone to heaven.
That song is my number one favorite of all time, and the
duo killed it, absolutely killed it. Everybody seemed to
think so. Except Zane.

He was in the same position he had kept from the
start, phone in front of his face—not moving, not singing,
not talking, not dancing. Was he breathing? Who knew?
Apparently, recording the event for some nameless posterity was more important. He was having a completely
non-participatory, second-hand experience of one of
the greatest concerts ever. That irritated the crap out of
me. Letting him interfere with my own good time was a

shame, but it did. My inner attitude was once again, "he's not acting like my ideal boyfriend/suitor/rock fan." That, of course, was my own fantasy to get over. Partly, any old fashioned Southern woman feels some obligation to make sure her date is having a good time. Rooted to the ground like an automaton, he surely didn't seem to be.

Sacrificing a few seconds of "Wild Horses," I turned and yelled into Zane's ear, "Wow, this is incredible! I think you'd really love to see it for real, without your phone." If looks could kill, I would be dead.

"Why don't you stop videoing for a minute?"

Zane didn't even answer, just swung back around, lifting the phone to eye level in one smooth motion.

You can't say I didn't try. Time to throw in the towel. Maybe his phone battery would die and he would have to join in the fun.

Didn't happen. Either his phone had the world's most energetic battery or Zane spent part of the concert watching through a dead device. He did not lower the phone for one single moment, not for "Honky Tonk Women," not for Springsteen in "Tumbling Dice," not for the encores, not even for the introduction of the band, not for anything.

Catching glimpses through my binoculars, I soaked up the thunderous vibrations, screamed myself hoarse, and danced 'til I was ready to drop. Loving every minute of the show and wishing it would go on for hours, sadly it finally ended, and as we filed out, the people around me were all on a high, same as me. Maybe the high was chemical for some, but for me, the show itself was buoyant enough.

After we reached the exit to our section, Zane grabbed my arm and dragged me through the crowd. Where were we going? Still in a daze, I stumbled along, bumping into other happy concert-goers. Once outside, the shock of the cold brought me back to reality. Zane deposited me next to a tree with a tense, "Stay here. I'm going to buy some mementos."

"If I give you money will you get me a couple of t-shirts, size large?" One for me and one for my son, Daniel, was plenty, since they probably cost a fortune.

"Yeah, you can pay me back when I know how much they are. I'll be back in a while."

A while turned into forty-five minutes of dancing around to keep out the cold and de-briefing with other fans hanging around the tree. One of those was a guy who hung around longer than the others, so when Zane finally returned, he was unpleasantly surprised to find me deep in conversation with a strapping young stud. Zane grabbed my arm and promptly hustled me away from my new friend. Apparently, conversation with another male was enough of a defection to send Zane back over the edge. Can you say bayonet knife? His expression was unpleasantly similar to that of the moment when I had looked at him the wrong way on that street corner in Manhattan. The set of his mouth and the distant cast of his eyes signaled that the man was *not* pleased. Ugh, not again, especially not after such an enjoyable concert. This was not something I was in the mood to confront, but I sighed and attempted to jolly Zane out of his doldrums.

"Hey, can I see what you bought? There must have been hundreds of people in line."

He didn't respond well to the jollity. "Just wait 'til we get on the train, can you? It's not a good idea to pull everything out here."

"Yeah, sure," I said. "You bought a ton. Was it expensive?"

"A fortune," he said. "Just like the concert, not worth it."

A number of responses came to mind:

(a) "Then why'd you come?"

(b) "By 'not worth it,' are you referring to me?"

(c) "How do you know, since you didn't see the concert except through your phone?"

(d) "Do you enjoy being such an asshole?"

(e) All of the above.

Mindful of still being broke in New Jersey, those thoughts went unspoken. Instead, I kept to the high ground with a nondescript "Mmmm" and a neutral glance.

We kept a careful distance from each other as we walked toward the train station. After a couple of minutes, my good mood reasserted itself, and I began to sing lines from "Gimme Shelter." When I got to, "it's just a kiss away, it's just a kiss away," Zane gave me *that* look. Not the scary one. Seriously? He acts like a jerk, but mention the word "kiss" and all of a sudden he's amorous? He had another thing coming.

Or did he? As Zane nudged my back to the wall and leaned in to kiss me, I felt a bulge in his pocket. Borrowing from Mae West's famous line, was that a Bayonet knife in his pocket or was he just glad to see me?[133]

Making a quick judgment that discretion was the better part of valor, I let him kiss me. It was not a very stirring kiss, sort of a half-hearted "I'm a guy and I know I'm supposed to do this" kind of kiss, and after a moment we broke apart and continued our walk. The knife was still an open question, so I redoubled my efforts to create a good atmosphere between us. The kiss had helped, and now our walk felt more companionable.

After a few more minutes we arrived at the Newark station and, first lucky break of the night, the train pulled in a moment later. We boarded and grabbed a couple of seats, then Zane put his bag of mementos on his lap and proceeded to show me the treasure trove. God knows how much he had spent on memorabilia for a concert he'd barely even seen. It would give him bragging rights, anyway.

Short sleeved t-shirts, long-sleeved t-shirts, hooded sweatshirts, sweatshirts without hoods, badges, CDs—you name it, he had bought it. Zane produced two t-shirts for me, scoring a bull's-eye with a reissue of the old shirt with the big tongue from the inside sleeve of the 1971 Sticky Fingers album that later became the Stones' defining logo. We agreed to settle up the next day when I had cash. It was too much to fit in his suitcase, so we decided to pack

---

133 Famously bawdy in popular films of the 1930s, Mae West is known for many lines, among them, "Is that a gun in your pocket, or are you just glad to see me?"

Zane's considerable excess in my bag and divide everything up when we landed in Atlanta.

The rest of the train trip and cab ride home passed in a fog, with no thought of going down to the Village to listen to music. Mick and company had sated my appetite for sounds, and the stress of the afternoon had been wearing. To my relief, Zane seemed to feel the same, and we bid each other a cordial good night at the doors to our respective rooms.

CHAPTER FIVE

Get Thee Away from Me, Betty Boop!

Exhausted as I was, I slept like a log and woke feeling refreshed, hopeful even that the rest of the trip would coast by smoothly. Reaching for my cell phone, the screen showed that it was almost out of juice. Where was my charger? Nowhere to be found. The charger was in my hip pocket all day Saturday, but must have fallen out sometime during the concert, leaving me with a dying phone.

Maybe Zane has the same kind of charger, I thought. A quick text later, and Zane replied that, yes, he had a charger that would work, just come on by and borrow it. Great! It only took a moment for me to throw on jeans and a t-shirt and go knock politely at Zane's door. He opened it wide for an immediate view of...whoa there, cowboy. What a view, a view that gave new meaning to the expression ending with "...only a mother could love." Clad in his tidy whities and nothing else, his left arm stretched up the doorframe, right arm on his hip, head at a rakish (he thought) angle, Zane looked up through lowered eyelashes, a male version of Betty Boop.

For a moment, we both froze. It took a minute to process Zane's pose. In his case, perhaps he was waiting for me to drop my phone and, overwhelmed by desire, launch myself at the expanse of his bare midsection. For the sake of Zane's manhood, I'd love to report that I thought about it, but there was no whisper of sexual arousal. None. On the other hand, while Zane had misread my libido, he was dead on target with my funny bone. Snatching the charger he held aloft, I bolted out of the room, opened my door, and collapsed on the floor in gales of laughter. Zane's seduction failed, but I didn't want to hurt his feelings by letting him hear me laugh out loud. As soon as I could get up off the floor, I ran into the bathroom, sat on the toilet, flushed it, turned on the shower and the sink, and laughed out loud until tears ran down my cheeks, the best laugh I'd had in years. Forget Jagger, the laugh alone was enough to make the trip worthwhile.

Pulling myself together, I stripped and got in the shower, running the water hot then cold to compose myself. The flush in my cheeks had turned a rather dangerous purple from my fit of hysterics. Calmed and clean, I dressed again and texted Zane as if nothing had happened: "Hey, are you about ready for breakfast?"

Equally unperturbed, Zane replied, "Let's go, I'm starving!" We met in the hallway and headed out. Though the sky was overcast, the temperature had warmed up and it was pleasant enough strolling around the block. We found a welcoming diner with no waiting line, and for a change of pace, enjoyed the same breakfast of Challah bread French toast—his covered with powdered sugar then slathered with maple syrup, mine buried under a mountain of strawberry jam—and bacon and cheese omelets. The smells were sensational, all kinds of sugar overlaid with the pervasive scent of hot melted butter. Who could be in a bad mood in the middle of that?

After breakfast, back towards our hotel we came across the Tenement Museum, which told the story of families, mine included, who emigrated to America in the late nineteenth and early twentieth century and settled on the Lower East Side. I dragged Zane in for a tour, followed by a *long* visit to the gift shop.[134] Now I had my own shopping bags to contend with.

By the time we got back to the hotel, we had to pack up and leave for the airport. Zane brought me the items he was unable to fit in his bag and by dint of some expert

---

134 I am a museum gift shop aficionado: my favorite for gifts is the shop at the Chicago Museum of Contemporary Art and for books is the shop at the Michael C. Carlos Museum in Atlanta, each an absolute jewel.

folding and bundling, I succeeded in squeezing them in, as well as my new purchases. With plenty of time to spare, we met in the lobby to check out and call an Uber. The ride to the airport was unremarkable, other than the sight of an unconscious Santa or two sleeping it off in the occasional doorway. The stars seemed to be aligned, as even security at La Guardia was light. Headed to our gate, I thought about which fast food kiosk we should stop at for dinner. Since it was Sunday and Chick-fil-A was closed as usual, its shuttered gate beckoned like a siren. Isn't that always the way? I haven't eaten a fried chicken sandwich for years, but not a Sunday goes by that I don't look longingly at every Chick-fil-A I pass.

As we turned a corner, a sharp pain struck in the crease behind my left knee. Having endured the anxiety and discomfort of a blood clot a couple of years back, it scared the dickens out of me. In all innocence, I told Zane about it, not dreaming that he would shove me into the nearest chair, kneel down, fling my leg onto his lap, shove my pants up over my knee and start massaging my leg for all he was worth. It must have been that ersatz Navy Seal training taking over again. A crowd of curious onlookers gathered to inquire after my well-being while I made an emergency call to a doctor friend, who recommended baby aspirin. Gratefully I hobbled off to buy the aspirin, leaving one apparent kindred spirit in earnest discourse with Zane about the merits of various massage techniques. Good, I hoped she was hitting on him. Maybe we could trade seats if she was on our flight. That airport scene had worked my last nerve, and if I wasn't over Zane before he pulled that stunt, I was now.

No such luck. Upon my return, bottle of pills in hand, Zane awaited me *sans* kindred spirit.

Through power of suggestion or otherwise, the pain in my leg subsided after taking an aspirin and, the quest for dinner abandoned, we boarded the plane without further disruption. In fact, an atmosphere of calm descended as we took off, and soon we were both reading books, munching on as many pretzels and peanuts as we could snag from the flight attendant. Midway through the flight, the captain announced that there was stormy weather the rest of the way into Atlanta and cabin service would be discontinued. That was okay, I couldn't have eaten another crunchy snack if I'd tried. Zane turned to me and said, "Darn, I hate for my son to have to pick us up in bad weather."

That was the first I'd heard about his son. It was news to me that Zane even had a son living in the Atlanta area. Whether that was a deliberate omission on Zane's part or failure to inquire on mine wasn't clear. No matter, I was happy to have a ride home in the rain.

"I didn't realize you were planning on giving me a ride. Thanks!"

Zane nodded and we both returned to our books until we landed and the plane coasted to a stop at our gate. Disembarking, naturally we found ourselves at the last gate on the concourse, farthest from the train that would take us to baggage claim, but I didn't mind. We were on the home stretch! I could almost taste the air in my apartment, so peaceful and relaxing, Augie on my lap.[135]

At baggage claim, we grabbed our luggage, mine heavy with the spoils of Zane's concert memorabilia, and my purchases at the museum gift shop. Out on the sidewalk, I asked, "Why don't we open our bags and transfer the concert stuff that I packed to your suitcase?"

Could someone please tell me what is wrong with that question? To this day, I can't figure out what part of my simple request sent Zane into orbit. Unlike his earlier reactions—a little frozen contempt—this was at the other end of the spectrum. Think volcanic anger, on the order of Krakatoa or Mt. St. Helens.

Snapping out his words, Zane said, "Can't. You. Just. Wait Until. We. Get. To. The. Car?" This string of words was accompanied by a glare that can only be described as withering.

"Uh, sure," I replied, staring at my feet.

The silence continued until a car pulled up to the curb. A young man jumped out, someone I would have known anywhere as Zane's son. They were remarkably alike in looks and gesture, though on the surface the kid seemed a lot more amiable. Zane managed to pull himself together and introduce me to his son, David, then yanked open our suitcases to accomplish the transfer that had provoked such outrage.

---

135 Thanks to the best pet sitters in the world, Augie and Ace would be waiting for me when I got home. If you live in Atlanta, call me for their numbers. Sometimes I get the feeling that Ace likes them a whole lot more than me, that's how good they are. And how fickle cats are.

"How much do I owe you?"

"A hundred and twenty dollars should cover it," Zane replied. They weren't giving away those t-shirts.

Taking the money from my wallet, I handed it to Zane and climbed into the back seat of his son's Honda Civic. The car looked like it had been through the wars, with dings and dents all down the passenger side. Never mind. All it had to do was deliver me to my house in one piece. Famous last words.

Zane took the driver's seat and David went around to the other side. Off we went. In the wrong direction. In the driving rain. In the pitch-black dark since, inexplicably, all of the streetlights seemed to be off. After a few moments of gathering my courage, I said, "Uh, Zane, I live the other way. You know, north of the city, and right now we're going south."

Zane swerved to the side, fishtailed into a U-turn half and got us headed back in the right direction. He was angry, really angry. It wasn't clear exactly what had triggered his black mood, and it really didn't matter. Just get me home.

Home. Did I really want Zane to know exactly where I lived? He knew the community, but I'd given him no address. That's how I was going to keep it.

"Hey, Zane, you know what? I'm going to stay over at my cousin's tonight. Let me give you her address." My cousin had a building that was staffed by a concierge 24/7 and that suited me fine right about then.

Zane drove faster and faster, tailgating other cars and swerving in and out of traffic. Typical of Atlanta, cars were thick even on a Sunday night at 11:45 p.m. In desperation, I made light conversation with David, attempting to elevate Zane's mood, but even David replied only with monosyllables and grunts. Had his father somehow telegraphed the message, "Do not under any circumstances be friendly to Lynn?" It sure felt that way. By the time we arrived at my cousin's building, my neck was tight and shoulders frozen from holding them rigid the entire ride. Holding my breath, I rang the night bell and waited for the concierge, who to my relief showed up right away, a little startled when I practically jumped into his arms.

"Good night, Zane, thanks for everything, it was really a great time, boy was that a great concert," I babbled, praying that he would just leave.

"Bye," he said. A man of few words, he turned on his heel and left. Thank you, God.

Leaning weakly against the wall, I took out my phone and called yet another Uber. Fifteen minutes away, but who cared? Still miraculously in one piece, I soon would be in my apartment, all by my lonesome. Going into detail about the whole bad date thing to the concierge seemed pointless, so we chatted about nothing until the Uber arrived.

At 12:20 a.m. the driver pulled into the cul-de-sac where my unit was located. Grateful beyond measure to be home safe and sound, I left him possibly the biggest tip on record for an Uber driver, raced through the door to greet Augie and Ace, and fell straight into my bed.

The next day, I edited myself out of the shot the drunk Santa lady had taken of Zane and me in New York and printed a copy at work. Dropping a nice big color photo of Zane off at the security gate at my complex, I explained to the guard on duty, "If you see a guy who looks like this, do *not* let him in. Okay?"

"Okay."

"This is a man I went out with, and I think he might not be a totally safe person, you know what I mean?"

"Yeah, I get it."

"Please pass it around to the other guards, okay?'

"Okay."

Who knew if they would heed my warnings? That was the best I could do for the moment. Longer term, it was time to re-think this whole dating thing.

CODA

If at this point you are pounding the table, scaring the crap out of the dog and yelling, "Didn't that dumb bitch learn anything?"—fear not. As the official recipient of the "dumbest smart person anyone knows" award, I have, as you will recall, two terminally inconsistent sides. Part of me even now *would* probably take a trip to Bora Bora with a relative stranger hoping that we would end up life partners. And still wonder what went wrong when I got stranded on a reef in the Pacific with nothing but some salted fish and a bottle of Orange Crush to tide me over until I was rescued.

Fortunately, I do have another side. To soothe your jangled nerves, read on for a coda from grown up, therapy-adjusted, wise, reflective, and self-aware Lynn. Or if you are charmed by the idea of a senior citizen tilting at windmills like a female Don Quixote without apology, feel free to close this book and remember her only.

LESSONS LEARNED

L ife is a funny thing. In what euphemistically might be called mid-to-late middle age,[136] I get upset when my children don't leap to help me lift suitcases and carry packages up the steps, each of the three often remarking, "Mom, you're acting like you're eighty and you're not!" Then I realize that their attitude is a compliment, and when the time comes that they do assume that I need help, I will be sad because it will mean in their eyes I am too old to do these things for myself. Sometimes it feels that life is a matter of chasing something that is always out of reach.

Like dating: a good thing that is always just out of reach. The sequence that began with Allen and culminated with Zane[137] left me exhausted and, for a while, questioning my sanity. One definition of insanity is "doing the same thing

---

136   According to Wikipedia, the Oxford English Dictionary defines middle age as between 45 and 65. "The period between early adulthood and old age, usually considered as the years from about 45 to 65." The US Census lists the category middle age as being from 45 to 65. Merriam-Webster lists middle age from 45 to 64. https://en.wikipedia.org/wiki/Middle_age

From now on, I'll be looking elsewhere for my definitions, *ergo*

https://www.psychologytoday.com/us/blog/constructive-wallowing/201801/could-60-be-the-new-40

137   Allen to Zane, "A to Z," get it?

over and over and expecting different results."[138] Sound apropos? All those dates, the outcomes the same, leaving me with funny stories featuring knives, guns, and multi-legged insects, but little else. All those dating websites, all those times gearing up to flirt at the grocery at the end of a long day's work—thinking "Shit, my feet hurt," while whinnying, "Oh, looks like you're getting ready for a party. I just love that wine!" Nothing to show for it.

Should I give up for good? Be alone, stay alone, live alone, give in and become the cat lady, or in my case, the dog and cat lady? Logically, that made sense, and for a time, I did choose that path—just gave up and gave in to the idea that I would be alone. Initially, it was a delight. Not searching for the latest clever club to join in order to meet men—après ski, anyone? Oh, that's right, we live in Georgia—was so restful. Choosing the opposite of anything works well when you're rebounding from an unpleasant or taxing situation. Quitting a job you hate produces an immediate reaction of bliss. But unemployment as bliss only works for a while. Until the boredom and lack of purpose, not to mention financial instability, set in. When my kids grew up and moved out, the peace was wonderful, the lack of responsibility heaven...until I missed them so much it hurt, and I nearly lost myself in the void of their absence.

---

138 http://professorbuzzkill.com/einstein-insanity-qnq/ Some interesting controversy surrounds this quote (https://www.psychologytoday.com/us/blog/in-therapy/200907/the-definition-insanity-is), but as applied to my own actions, it is solid.

What about sex? In the old days, the lack of sex, or at least the pursuit of it, would have been a deal breaker. Perhaps that was based on a deep conviction that I wasn't a woman unless proving it romantically and sexually. Hence, in part, the series of unfortunate events I've described. Aside from wanting sex, missing it, needing it or even feeling desire, getting sex became a box to check off for happiness. It took a while to figure out that this was backwards thinking. If the men I met were not a fit for me, nothing could be gained by pretending otherwise, or by trying to manufacture lust out of thin air. The only thing gained was some raw body parts and a bruised ego. Not much value in that.

So: no men and no sex, other than with my patiently waiting neon pink Bombex vibrator.[139] Was this, then, the end of the line? Give up dating and embrace being single forever? Part of me would have been content to say yes and spend the rest of my life with my friends, children, dog and cat, perhaps a late-in-life exotic animal or two[140] to spice things up. But eventually the pleasures of aloneness drifted into the discomfort of loneliness, and that was intolerable.

Loneliness really sucks. For me, isolation is the spider at the center of the web of depression. Any inkling of that spider flexing its hairy little muscles sends off all kinds of alarms in my head. While I have regained stability in recent years, a big chunk of my earlier days was spent

---

139   Remember my "Trusted Life Partner" from note 21? Still the same one. Men may come and go, but vibrators stick around.

140   Still thinking about those wonderful seahorses. They might make good pets.

battling depression, and descent into that particular hell is not something to risk in any way.

So what's the answer? For me, great answers are in short supply. Even good answers are hard to come by. The template that I live by was set in stone a long, long time ago, and as I said at the outset, I drank the Kool-Aid in a big way. With full awareness of every lousy date and every crummy experience and of my own rather substantial shortcomings, I still believe that romance is possible and that Mr. Right might be around the next corner. Witness a recent exchange with my son about my younger daughter and her boyfriend:

Me: "You know, Rose wants to go to law school, but she's only looking in New Orleans because of Keigan."

Daniel: "What? They've only been dating for four months."

Me: "Yeah, but they are really in love."

Daniel: "What do you think this is, *Romeo and Juliet*? They've been dating a few months! Are you out of your mind?"

Daniel had a point of course, and I had to laugh. But maybe I did, too. Time will tell for Rose. As for me, I'm a Southern woman. Have you ever known any Southern women? We don't give up. Ever. We're stubborn.

Not that I haven't learned a couple of things. Not that I haven't traded the Kool-Aid for Crystal Light; give me a little credit. The diet of outlandish romance novels my mother fed me through my formative years no longer provides the narrow lens through which I view my potential counterparts. Back then, I wasn't aware enough to know that none of the drivel in those novels is true. My boy-friend was supposed to be the Scarlet Pimpernel,[141] a composite of every hero, known or imagined, lumped into one impossible standard. The list of qualifications Mr. Right had to meet are embarrassing to recall. Forget tall, raven haired, and broad in the chest; those were a given. Funny, smart, clever, witty, well-traveled, accomplished, well read, sports fan, sophisticated, manly, take charge, family oriented, caring, introspective, and intuitive.

That's only a partial list.

Believe it or not, there were plenty of dates. Even as a ridiculously picky girl, not to mention shy, and subject to mood swings, and self-imposed isolation, in the best of times I came off as whimsical, fun loving, smart, and sophisticated. So guys came and went, mostly went. In my fantasy world, fights, arguments, and fundamental differences weren't supposed to happen, so when they happened in real life, I simply ended the relationship. Three months was a victory.

By sheer luck, my future—now former—husband appeared in law school and we married when I was in my early thirties. Even though adulthood had made me aware that Baroness Orczy's[142] imagination was not the best

---

141 Think of Rhett Butler, Zorro, Superman, Tarzan, and Sir Lancelot rolled into one, swooping in on a white stallion, dismounting, and brewing me a cup of tea to ease my monthly cramps. The Scarlet Pimpernel was the perfect man, existing only in his author's imagination and my mother's— and under her tutelage my own—fantasies. If you want to take a break from reality and visit la la land, here's your chance: Emmuska Orczy, Baroness. *The Scarlet Pimpernel*. London, England: Hodder and Stoughton, 1905.

142 See n. 141.

guide to my romantic life, I entered the marriage without knowing much about relationships. Marriage required a lot of learning during the nineteen years Wayne and I were together, principally on the reality front. Accepting balance and compromise and that flesh and blood men are just like me, imperfect, and best of all, human, took a lot of trial and error. My memories of the first year of marriage are peppered with uncharacteristic drama, like throwing pots of rice at him and grandly exiting the car in the middle of nowhere, only to get back inside ten cold and rainy minutes later. Nineteen years later, I had learned quite a bit, just not quite enough to equip me for the dating scene. Perhaps that's because I began the journey with such a long way to go. Or perhaps it is because the dating scene is truly, genuinely, irrevocably screwed up. Probably a little bit of both.

Okay, so I had a bunch of lousy dates and it's taking *a lot* longer than I thought to find a guy who "gets" me and wants to be with me, flaws and all. Is life always going to be a matter of chasing something that is just out of reach, like those poor greyhounds chasing the mechanical rabbit at the dog races?[143] It's true, sometimes I do feel that way.

---

143   Can you believe it? Not a month after I wrote this, the news media reported that Florida had just outlawed greyhound racing. https://www.nytimes.com/2018/11/09/us/greyhound-racing-florida-adoption.html. Good for the greyhounds, and I hope they all get adopted quickly. Supposedly, despite being really fast and bred to race, they are total couch potatoes at home and make sweet, low-maintenance pets.

My analogy, on the other hand, is totally shot. And it was perfect. There isn't another analogy so perfect. Even the damn analogy is just out of reach.

Point made.

Yet I also have the sense that I'm getting closer and closer to catching the rabbit. Change is in the air, and maybe my time is just around the corner.

In the meantime, I've got a Plan A and a Plan B. Sitting and waiting for the phone to ring is not part of either. Plan B first. While I'm not sitting by the phone, if you happen to know a great single guy, do me a favor and tell him to call me. Plan A? I'd tell you about Plan A, but then I'd have to kill you, and I've grown to like you even if you didn't read all of the footnotes.

ACKNOWLEDGMENTS

I would like to acknowledge contributions made by so many people. First, my professional editor, David Darracott, for making critical changes without which the book would have fallen flat. David was selected as the well-deserved 2015 Author of the Year by the Georgia Writers Association and is the leader of my writers' group, without whom the book would have never been completed. Superb writers all, they pushed, pulled, prodded, and poked until I wrote the best book possible. Beside David, they include Rona Simmons, Michael Mollick, Michael Geoghegan, and Michelle Valigursky. Friends and family, all non-professionals with a superb talent for critiquing, gave me feedback that had tremendous impact on the final manuscript. My friends Keith Friedlander, Nancy Ghertner, Elizabeth Murray, and Gretchen Lefever Watson all made cogent comments that led me to re-shape numerous passages in the book. Cathie Sekendur deserves special mention, reading the manuscript several times, and pointing out elements that the book was better off without. Lindsay Scarff Goodman, my daughter-in-law, caught internal inconsistencies and jarring notes that nobody else did, and has a brilliant editing career in front of her should she choose to pursue it. The proofreading talents of three wonderful copy editors spared me the ignominy of a book sprinkled with mistakes. The first two are Uli Guthrie and Hannah Wood, both consummate professionals. The third is my daughter, Rose Goodman, who might also have a career in the book business if she weren't on her way to law school.

On the creative side, I owe a huge debt of gratitude to my daughter, Jean Baker—who says writing isn't a family affair?—who had just launched her eponymous photography business in Richmond, and made my author's photograph a big win for someone who is not known for being photogenic. Many, many thanks also to Greg Houston, for so willingly accommodating this project during the holiday season and creating the terrific illustration for the cover of the book. I likewise owe a tremendous debt of gratitude to Chris Falkenstein, the most responsive and talented website designer who ever lived, as well as the most irreverent, which suits me well. Chris also rescued me from floundering in the SEO world by recommending Justin Iannaco, who did a superb job while never making me feel stupid for my ignorance in technical matters. Many thanks also to Amanda Matthews at AM Design Studios for the perfect book cover, Jessica Ess at Hillspring Books for doing an outstanding job on interior design and book formatting, Carol Hoenig for her wise counsel on publicity, and Linda Ingroia for her experience and skill as a copy writer. As for marketing, how lucky could I get? I would have been lost without the supremely talented Julie Trelstad, who put together the most up-to-date, creative, and intelligent marketing plan imaginable, and her staff: Alexandra Battey, Mandy McClelland and Linsday Davis. *Sex and the Single Grandma* is the product of a true collaboration among all of these wonderful folks, and just goes to show that you can still create something grand with an intimate network of like-minded, talented people.

Special thanks goes to the women who shared the "random online dating messages" that gave such spice to the book's "Interludes." Ladies, we're all in this together.

Finally, I would like to express my heartfelt appreciation to all of my friends, who walk through the fire with me all the time without complaint. Although I'd like to think so, I doubt very much that I am low maintenance.